Aunt,

Thank you for stopping to speak with me! I pray you ask God to show you what He wants you to see, know —

Blessings,
Janice

# Journey
## to your
# Calling

THE Book You DO!!!

# Journey
## to your
## Calling

### The Path To Receive
### The Desires of Your Heart

**Janice Hatcher Liggins**

XULON PRESS

Xulon Press
2301 Lucien Way #415
Maitland, FL 32751
407.339.4217
www.xulonpress.com

Unless otherwise indicated, Scripture quotations taken from the King James Version (KJV)—*public domain.*

Scripture quotations taken from the New King James Version (NKJV). Copyright © 1982 by Thomas Nelson, Inc. Used by permission. All rights reserved.

Printed in the United States of America.

Paperback ISBN-13: 978-1-6322-1590-1
eBook ISBN-13: 978-1-6322-1591-8

# WHAT PRE-RELEASE READERS HAVE SAID

"If you are looking for a book that will answer some of your questions concerning God's plan for your life and how to seek answers from the Lord, I highly recommend this book to you." *Rev. Diana P. Cherry, church administrator emerita, From the Heart Church Ministries Worldwide*

***

"What an inspired work! I enjoyed reading it, and I am so pleased to be among your first literary fans!" *Dr. Christopher Loffredo, professor at Georgetown University, former neighbor*

***

"It's a really good how-to book. It has very specific and practically laid-out ways to have a life with God. Your fervor, of course, comes through." *Regina L., music director, "Mrs. B's" daughter*

***

"*Journey to Your Calling* is presented in a personalized way that is challenging and thought provoking.

Over the years I have received wise advice from parents, elders and mentors but never have I received the advice, "Anything you hear me say, you can say. Anything you see me do, you can do. And, anywhere you see me go, you can go". I certainly have never been bold enough to give such advice to anyone. Journey to Your Calling is a user's guide to life; it challenges me to heighten my level of commitment.

I grew up hearing the expression, "Trust and obey" (the LORD). It was a paradigm shift for me to consider, "Obey and then trust", as presented in Journey to Your Calling.

I have often heard people quote Psalms 37:4 "Delight thyself also in the LORD; and he shall give thee the desires of thine heart". Before reading Journey to Your Calling, I never would have considered that it is through being completely submissive to GOD's will that HIS will becomes my will and the desires of HIS heart becomes the desires of my heart." *Bro. Don Turner, member From the Heart Church Ministries*

\*\*\*

"Do yourself a favor and read this book! You will be inspired, encouraged, and motivated to pursue God's plan for your life, and you will be immensely blessed in the process!" *Kia Liggins Braxton, Janice Hatcher Liggins' daughter*

\*\*\*

"This project was a breeze because you are a good writer, and I was blessed by the contents." *Sister Toni Foxx, first* Journey *editor, executive assistant (retired), From the Heart Church Ministries*

\*\*\*

"The author uses Scripture references effectively in relaying the importance of being saved by Jesus and then continuing on in spiritual maturity to grasp all that God has for you on your spiritual journey. The use of the Bible allows readers to see Scripture as relevant to their journey; that Scripture is able to answer questions they may have on what God is doing in their lives and how He is directing them. These are common questions believers, and even non-believers, might have."
*Salem Authors, publisher*

***

# DEDICATION

I dedicate this book to the two men who had the greatest impact on my life: my father and my pastor.

Deacon Nathaniel A. & Annie R. Hatcher

**I dedicate this book to my earthly father, Deacon Nathaniel A. Hatcher, Sr. — my dad, my example, my teacher, my silent business partner, and my best friend.** My father was the most righteous man I have ever known, bar none. He was a living epistle, seen and read by all men. He loved the Lord, and everyone who knew him knew that without him ever preaching a word. My father lived the Bible. He was an excellent father to his nine children and a wonderful husband to his wife, Annie Ruth Harling Hatcher, mother of his nine children. There are eight girls and one boy; I am girl number three. The boy is next to the baby, and yes, that only boy was — and is — spoiled rotten!

My father was an excellent example to his children. When I was 14 years old, Daddy took the oldest four girls aside and charged us, saying, **"Anything you hear me say, you can say. Anything you see me do, you can do. And anywhere you see me go, you can go."** At 14, I must tell you, I had absolutely no appreciation for the magnitude of the commitment within his charge. However, years later, after I got married and had my own children, I realized that his charge reflected the awesome commitment my father made to his children and lived before us!

Daddy purchased six acres of land in Lanham, Maryland, when I was just two years old. Later, he purchased two adjoining acres, then owning eight contiguous acres. He built our mom the home of her dreams, sitting in the middle of a two-acre clearing. My father wanted to develop the property, but with raising nine children, his energy and finances went towards caring for his family. After he passed and just before my mom passed, Mom had an attorney draw up a trust agreement; the land now belongs to the trust. I am one of three sibling trustees, appointed in the trust by Mom. I am also the business manager for the trust and for the land development project. I am committed to carrying out my father's vision to develop the property. The family has agreed that whatever type of project we build, it will carry the name "Hatcher's Haven." We will include a family archive on the property to honor Mom and Dad. All my siblings agree. We are delighted to do so.

Founding Pastor John A. & Rev. Diana P. Cherry

**I dedicate this book also to Dr. John A. Cherry, Founder and Episcopal Pastor of From the Heart Church Ministries Worldwide.** Pastor Cherry was the boldest teacher of the Gospel I have ever heard! He taught the Truth, whether you liked it or not. He would teach, "If I can't show it to you in the Bible, don't believe me." He was also the most obedient Christian I have ever known. Whatever the Lord told Pastor to do, he did it, boldly. During one of his Pastors and Leaders Institutes, I witnessed Pastor give the call to Christ to a room full of other pastors. I was stunned! Yet, nearly 50 men, pastors and leaders, went to the altar. Yes, Pastor Cherry was indeed bold and obedient. In just 35 years, From the Heart grew to a global footprint with multiple From the Heart churches on nearly every continent and numerous churches throughout the United States. Each church originated by the interest of people who wanted to be a part of From the Heart Church Ministries. This includes pastors who gave up rights to churches they had started to become a From the Heart church. I got saved at Trinidad Baptist Church, but my personal relationship with the Lord, to know God for myself, came through teachings at From the Heart. I learned the ways of God, how to keep my heart pure, and how to think correctly.

I say, From the Heart teaches the "straight and narrow!" If you want to stay right with God, From the Heart is an excellent place to learn how.

*Journey to Your Calling*

## GREETINGS FRIEND...

I wanted to share a little background of the book prior your reading of it.

It was not my idea to write this book. The Lord told me to "Write a book." He even gave me the title of the book. The title meant nothing to me at the time. I immediately said, "Lord I have nothing to tell the people, so I ask YOU to write the book through me." And He did... Ideas flowed constantly for three weeks, then they stopped. I had captured pages and pages of scribbled ideas. I organized the ideas into groups; those groups became my chapters; the chapters served as my Table of Contents. The entire book was outlined cover-to-cover, before I wrote the first sentence. I wrote every day for six months to finish the first rough draft. I read over what had been written. It was then that the title – the meaning of the book - registered for me.

The Lord has placed each of us on this planet for us to carry out our own specific, unique, and individual Assignment, or task. However, most people live and die, and never know what their Assignment was. I believe the Lord wanted this book in the earth because too many people live and die, never knowing why He sent them to this earth.

The purpose of this book is to serve as your guidebook on how to journey to your calling; how to identify and fulfill the Assignment God placed you on earth to carry out.

## NOTE:

In the original publishing of the book, though the Lord gave me the title "Journey to Your **Calling**," I often used the term 'purpose.' We are so regimented to the term Purpose. He has shown me there is a distinct difference between our Purpose, and our Calling.

# Journey to Your Calling

PURPOSE: As a Christian, we ALL have the same purpose. Our collective purpose is four-fold:

- to be Christ-like (so others can see Christ through us),
- to be salt in the earth
- to be light in the world to show the way for others, and
- to walk in our ministry of reconciliation; to lead others to Christ.

CALLING: Your Calling has nothing to do with your choice; nothing to do with your choice of education, career, employment, residence, or who you chose to marry. These were Your choices. Your calling is, "What did God choose for you? Why did He put you on to this planet?" The Lord has uniquely gifted and equipped you and each person, naturally and spiritually, for the Assignment He wants you to carry out.

As you Journey to **Your** Calling remember:

- Your Journey is with the Lord.
- This book is your roadmap.
- The Holy Spirit is your GPS.

He will lead, guide, strengthen, and prepare you for each level of spiritual maturity that is required for you to ultimately perform the Assignment the Lord has Called you to do.

May the Blessings of the Lord be upon you as you Journey to YOUR Calling!

I'd love to hear your feedback. Be sure to reach out!
**Website:** www.JourneyToYourCalling.com (Flip-Book, Podcast, sign up for Journey classes)
**Email:** Author@JourneyToYourCalling.com (Comments/Questions?)
BLESSINGS!   In His Service, Janice Hatcher Liggins

# TABLE OF CONTENTS

Foreword . . . . . . . . . . . . . . . . . . . . . . . . . . . . . . . . . . . . . . . . .xvii
Preface . . . . . . . . . . . . . . . . . . . . . . . . . . . . . . . . . . . . . . . . . . . xxi
Introduction . . . . . . . . . . . . . . . . . . . . . . . . . . . . . . . . . . . . xxvii

**1. Beyond Salvation** . . . . . . . . . . . . . . . . . . . . . . . . . . . . . . . . . . 1
   a. Born of His Spirit . . . . . . . . . . . . . . . . . . . . . . . . . . . . . . . . . 1
   b. Filled with His Spirit . . . . . . . . . . . . . . . . . . . . . . . . . . . . . . .5
   c. Led by His Spirit . . . . . . . . . . . . . . . . . . . . . . . . . . . . . . . . 10
   d. Member of the Body of Christ . . . . . . . . . . . . . . . . . . . . . . .14

**2. Establish a Relationship with the Lord** . . . . . . . . . . . . . . . .17
   a. Develop Your Prayer Life . . . . . . . . . . . . . . . . . . . . . . . . . 20
   b. Seek the Lord, Resist the Devil . . . . . . . . . . . . . . . . . . . . .29
   c. Promises with Conditions . . . . . . . . . . . . . . . . . . . . . . . . .33
   d. Recognize God's Voice . . . . . . . . . . . . . . . . . . . . . . . . . . . .37

**3. Allow God to Mature You** . . . . . . . . . . . . . . . . . . . . . . . . . . .41
   a. PURGE, PRUNE and PERFECT . . . . . . . . . . . . . . . . . . . .41
   b. PURGE: . . . . . . . . . . . . . . . . . . . . . . . . . . . . . . . . . . . . . . .42
      i. Renew Your Mind . . . . . . . . . . . . . . . . . . . . . . . . . . . .42
      ii. Stubbornness and Rebellion . . . . . . . . . . . . . . . . . . . . .44
      iii. Free Will . . . . . . . . . . . . . . . . . . . . . . . . . . . . . . . . . . .45
      iv. Possess Your Reins, Control Your Flesh . . . . . . . . . . . . . .47
   c. PRUNE . . . . . . . . . . . . . . . . . . . . . . . . . . . . . . . . . . . . . . 50

    i.  Come OUT of the World . . . . . . . . . . . . . . . . . . . . . . . . . 50

    ii. Grow up into Him. . . . . . . . . . . . . . . . . . . . . . . . . . . . . .59

    iii.Trust and Obey . . . . . . . . . . . . . . . . . . . . . . . . . . . . . . . 60

  d. PERFECT . . . . . . . . . . . . . . . . . . . . . . . . . . . . . . . . . . . . . .65

    i.  Guard Your Heart . . . . . . . . . . . . . . . . . . . . . . . . . . . . .65

    ii. Fasting . . . . . . . . . . . . . . . . . . . . . . . . . . . . . . . . . . . . . . .68

    iii.Righteousness . . . . . . . . . . . . . . . . . . . . . . . . . . . . . . . . . 70

    iv. Gifts of the Spirit: Walk in your Spiritual Gifts . . . . . . . . .73

**4. Allow God to Use You** . . . . . . . . . . . . . . . . . . . . . . . . . . . . . . .81

  a. When It Doesn't Make Sense (to Your Natural Mind) . . . . . . .82

  b. Ten Alligators Nipping at My Heels. . . . . . . . . . . . . . . . . . . . .96

  c. The Wilderness Experience . . . . . . . . . . . . . . . . . . . . . . . . . 104

  d. Look for the Good . . . . . . . . . . . . . . . . . . . . . . . . . . . . . . . 109

  e. The Desire of Your Heart . . . . . . . . . . . . . . . . . . . . . . . . . . 115

  f. Tribulations. . . . . . . . . . . . . . . . . . . . . . . . . . . . . . . . . . . . 118

**5. Fight the Good Fight of Faith** . . . . . . . . . . . . . . . . . . . . . . . . 125

  a. What Is Faith? . . . . . . . . . . . . . . . . . . . . . . . . . . . . . . . . . . 125

  b. Faith without Works Is Dead. . . . . . . . . . . . . . . . . . . . . . . . 128

  c. Today Is the Only Day Faith Will Work . . . . . . . . . . . . . . . . 132

  d. Embrace the Trials . . . . . . . . . . . . . . . . . . . . . . . . . . . . . . . 133

  e. When I Failed the Test . . . . . . . . . . . . . . . . . . . . . . . . . . . . 135

  f. Spiritual Barbells. . . . . . . . . . . . . . . . . . . . . . . . . . . . . . . . 139

  g. Fear. . . . . . . . . . . . . . . . . . . . . . . . . . . . . . . . . . . . . . . . . . 143

  h. Wrestle Not Against Flesh and Blood . . . . . . . . . . . . . . . . . 146

  i. Forgiveness . . . . . . . . . . . . . . . . . . . . . . . . . . . . . . . . . . . . 150

  j. Spiritual Warfare. . . . . . . . . . . . . . . . . . . . . . . . . . . . . . . . 153

  k. The Whole Armor of God . . . . . . . . . . . . . . . . . . . . . . . . . 156

**6. Love, the Greatest Commandment** . . . . . . . . . . . . . . . . . . . . 167

  a. Love God. . . . . . . . . . . . . . . . . . . . . . . . . . . . . . . . . . . . . . 167

b. Love Is the Greatest Gift ............................... 170

c. Love Your Brother ......................................171

d. Become Single and Complete in Jesus................... 175

e. Sacrifice................................................. 176

f. Be Content............................................. 178

g. Bear Fruit ............................................. 179

7. **Walk in Your Calling** ..................................... 185

a. Receive the Desires of Your Heart ...................... 186

b. Remain in Spiritual Perception ......................... 187

c. Recognize, Accept and Declare Your Calling ............. 194

d. Carry Out Your Assignment ........................... 196

e. Be Available to God .................................... 197

f. When God Pushes Pause............................... 199

g. Press Toward the Mark ................................ 203

h. Be Steadfast and Unmovable .......................... 205

What's Next? .............................................. 207

Acknowledgements ......................................... 209

The Clarion Call .......................................... 212

# Scripture Abbreviations

All Scriptures were taken from the King James Version,
unless otherwise indicated

| | |
|---|---|
| Acts | Acts |
| Cor | Corinthians |
| Chron | Chronicles |
| Deut | Deuteronomy |
| Eph. | Ephesians |
| Ex. | Exodus |
| Ez | Ezekiel |
| Gen. | Genesis |
| Jas | James |
| Jn. | John |
| 1Jn | 1 John |
| Jos | Joshua |
| Jer | Jeremiah |
| Jud | Judges |
| Heb | Hebrews |
| Hos | Hosea |
| Is | Isaiah |
| Luke | Luke |
| Mar | Mark |
| Matt | Mathew |
| NKJV | New King James Version |
| Pet | Peter |
| Phil. | Philippians |
| Ps | Psalms |
| Prov | Proverbs |
| Rom | Romans |
| Sam | Samuel |
| Tim. | Timothy |
| Thess | Thessalonians |

# FOREWORD

**Rev. Diana P. Cherry,** *Church Administrator Emerita,*
*FTHCM Worldwide*

Although JOURNEY TO YOUR CALLING chronicles the path that Sister Liggins travelled to reach and achieve the desires of her heart, I firmly believe this book can indeed be a guide or a road map for all of us to follow as we seek to find and to know God's plan, purpose, and Will for our own lives.

I am an avid reader; however, I do find it difficult to read many Christian books because they just tend to not hold my attention, and I lose interest in reading them. However, JOURNEY TO YOUR

CALLING was a blessing to me and also helpful to me, as I am now in a stage of life that I have NEVER had to face before! My husband made his transition to spend eternity with the Lord Jesus Christ. Therefore, I like many others, have found myself wondering about future directions for my life and ministry. Many of the situations that were shared in this book about the faithfulness of God were a source of encouragement to me and helped to remind me of the goodness and the faithfulness of our God!

This book is biblically based; however, the real-life experiences, problems, decisions and challenges faced by the writer make the book credible and exceptionally easy to read, digest, and enjoy. It is NOT a book that is so filled with Scriptures that one loses the "flow" of the life story! I truly appreciated reading the "personal" story, as the writer takes us on her journey with the Lord to reach her clarion call.

If you are looking for a book that will answer some of your questions concerning God's plan for your life and how to seek answers from the Lord, I highly recommend this book to you. You will learn seven important steps to follow as you begin the *Journey to Your Calling*:

1. You will be led to know what to expect beyond salvation.
2. You will be encouraged in how to establish a relationship with the Lord.
3. You will be encouraged to allow God to mature you.
4. You will be encouraged to allow God to use you.
5. You will be taught how to fight the good fight of faith.
6. You will learn that love is the Greatest Commandment.
7. You will be encouraged to walk in your calling.

As you begin your journey to God's plan and purpose for your life, may you always remember that obeying God is the first step in attaining a rewarded life in the Lord. When we obey, we are able to live in a blessed state, we build righteousness in our lives, and we put our faith into action and show the world that our God is God, and JESUS IS LORD!

God bless you and enjoy this book!

Rev. DIANA P. CHERRY
Church Administrator (Emerita)
From the Heart Church Ministries Worldwide®

# WHEN I LOOK BACK OVER MY LIFE, I SEE A STRAIGHT LINE

*I learned early in life to be confident in who I am, to be comfortable with ME.*

I was the third girl of eight, plus one boy who was next to the baby, in a loving and very close Christian family. I had an enchanted childhood. We celebrated every birthday (all eleven of us) every year. Christmas was exhilarating! We sang Gospel as a group, and we went to church every Sunday. My whole family is saved. My sisters were my friends and playmates. We did everything together. But I was different in many ways, and they would tease me about it — lovingly and never offensively, but tease, nonetheless. As young as age nine, they would tease me about being too dignified in how I acted, or too proper in simple things like the way I talked, or how my pinkie finger would stick out when I sipped from a cup. I did not mind their teasing because I liked the way I was; I liked the way I did things.

I thank God for preparing me to be comfortable with myself at a very early age, because in middle school, the comfort test really came, and it came hard. I was introduced to racism. Well, not actually introduced; it was just there, in my face, as a result of my choice. I had been bussed for miles to a particular junior/senior high school. It was a mammoth building built large enough to hold all the black students from miles and miles around. Junior high and senior high students co-existed, or at least they were in the same building — they did not co-exist. I hated it. As a seventh grader, I hated dealing with the rowdiness and bullying of the seniors. I pleaded with my parents to transfer me to the nearby middle school, which happened to be a white school. Some of my elementary school friends had already transferred there. My parents were concerned about the school because of racism, but I told them I would be all right; I had friends there. I did not expect the whites to like me, but at least they would be closer to my middle school age.

The whites didn't like me. They didn't like any of the other black students, for that matter. Black students were tolerated at best, mostly ignored, but frequently taunted. One of the most intriguing things that happened to me was with a student whom I considered friendly; her name was Diane. In home economics class, we had finished cooking and were cleaning the kitchen. Diane washed the dishes, and I was drying them. Suddenly, Diane stopped washing the dishes, took my hand, and with the dishcloth, she started scrubbing the back of my hand as rigorously as she could! I was stunned and puzzled for a moment. Then, I realized what she was trying to do. I told Diane that the brown was not dirt, it would not wash off, and it was the color of my skin. Diane was one of the whites I considered friendly. It is amazing the unkind things parents teach children at home.

Character tests, such as these, particularly in the pre-desegregation years, truly helped to refine my character, reaffirm my comfort with self, and prepare me for the continuing saga of life challenges to come.

***My dad was the most righteous man I have ever known.***

I was baptized in the Baptist Church when I was six years old. I knew it was a good thing to love the Lord. I didn't really love the Lord at six, but I knew that my parents loved Him, and I really loved them. My parents were my role models, particularly my dad. I learned to be a Christian by observing my dad. He was the epitome of meekness. He was a living epistle. He was the most righteous man I have ever known, bar none.

My dad always taught us that the oldest had to set the example for the younger siblings. However, though he never verbalized it this way, Jesus was his example, and Dad was our example (an example we could see). When I was 14, my dad gathered the four oldest girls together and began to give us guidance in a way he had never done before. We were 17, 15, 14 and 12. Dad gave us a charge and a commitment in three statements. He said: "Anything you hear me say, you can say. Anything you see me do, you can do. Anywhere you see me go, you can go."

At 14 years old, I didn't have very much appreciation for this charge because he only went to work and to church. What 14-year-old wants to do that? But, today, those words still echo in my heart. How awesome of a charge to give your teenage children, and then to live it! My dad lived it. Later, after getting married and becoming a parent myself, I must admit that I fell short of being able to live the same charge with my children. As I have watched them grow and have children of their own, I have developed an even more endearing appreciation for Dad's commitment to his children and to the Lord. I am grateful for the spiritual maturity of my dad when he made the charge. I am also truly grateful that I now have made this same charge to my grandchildren.

My mother was a mother to everyone who needed one. She was appointed mother of our Church, a position she held until her death. Our school friends and neighborhood friends would often play and eat at our house and would cry when it was time to go home. One of the most significant things my mother taught me was to look beyond a person's faults and to see their need. This wisdom still blesses me today.

### *The beginning of my spiritual journey: "How could he say that?"*

It was because of my father that I became determined to know the Lord for myself. When he became ill and needed surgery, we gathered for family prayer. Starting with the youngest, all on our knees, we took turns to pray, and we each prayed that God would guide the surgeon's hand and bless the surgery to go well. Daddy went last and also prayed that all would go well. But then he prayed, "Father, if it is not to be so, help my family to understand that it is really with You that I would rather be. Help my family to understand that I have lived all my life just for the day when I would see Your face." I was still kneeling. Stunned! Perplexed! **How could he say that?** Was he saying that he would rather be dead than to be with us? I knew my father well enough to know he loved us dearly, but I also knew he meant what he was saying. I HAD to know what would make him rather be dead than be with his family. My father knew something about the Lord that I didn't know. I was in my twenties during this prayer. My father's prayer sent me on a personal spiritual journey to seek the Lord for myself. I wanted to know the Lord like he did.

I sought the Lord; He heard me and answered me. I recognized His voice. I reached for Him and He guided me. The more I followed, the more He led. The more I gave Him credit for blessings, the more He blessed. I gave Him credit for everything. Then, credit turned to praise. The more I praised Him, the more of His power, grace and joy I felt. Then I worshiped Him and found His favor.

It was my father's steadfast and unfailing love for the Lord, demonstrated through his character, his conversation, and his actions, that caused me to start my personal search, my own spiritual journey. I wanted to know the Lord like my father knew Him.

Loving the Lord, looking beyond one's faults to see their need, meekness, and being a good example are strong foundational principles I learned from my parents that the Lord continues to use to further build and mold my character. They are forever with me at the core of who I am. These principles guide me in interactions with others, and they remind me that as a child of God, I must set the example for others. They transcend my personal relationships into any business relationship where they also serve me well.

***When I look back over my life, I see a straight line.***

When I look back over my life and my career, I see a straight line. Every position I have had was in direct preparation for the next; every project provided direct experience for the next to come. There are no deviations, no sidebars.

I did not realize it then, but the Lord has been preparing me all the while for this very point in time — my assignment to carry out the vision He has given me for The Clarion Call.

# INTRODUCTION

J ourney to Your Calling chronicles the seven major progressions of spiritual growth and development I experienced with the Lord on the journey to receiving my calling.

I believe each of us has a calling on our life. There is something the Lord wants each of us to do. We discover our calling after we have fully submitted our lives to the Lord and after we have been obedient and faithful in whatever tasks, steps, and actions the Lord gives us over the years.

We progress through life. I also believe each of us goes through the same Seven Progressions (or phases) of spiritual maturity as we individually journey to our calling. These are not my phases; they are phases of spiritual growth the Lord requires of each of us. The seven progressions outlined in this book apply to everyone, regardless of where your spiritual journey may take you or what incidents and challenges you may encounter along the way.

I share many personal experiences within each progression of my journey. However, my specific experiences and the incidents that occurred with me will likely not happen with you. My examples are unique to what the Lord wanted ME to learn and experience. I share very personal experiences only to give examples of the faithfulness of the Lord in bringing me through a challenge or presenting me with an opportunity. Your experiences and the incidents you encounter along your journey will be unique to you. Your experiences will be reflect what the Lord wants YOU to learn, the growth He wants you to make, and the assignments He wants you to carry out.

I have also incorporated several prayers the Lord gave me, which I have used over the years that have been a blessing to me. Please feel free to use them, or not. Change them, alter them, or use your own, as the Lord leads. The prayers are examples. Your prayers and responses may be unique to you.

I trust you will receive what the Lord has for you in reading this book. As you read this book I encourage you to ask the Lord to speak to your heart regarding everything He wants you to see, know and do.

May the blessings of the Lord be upon you.

Janice Hatcher Liggins

*Chapter 1*

# BEYOND SALVATION

S alvation is the very first step on a long journey home for the Christian. Heaven is our home. We are simply pilgrims here on earth, traveling through this distant land. Salvation is the only option available to make it back home to our Heavenly Father. Many people believe that being saved is all they need to do to get to Heaven. And that is true if your only interest is getting into Heaven when you die. However, what does the Lord want you to do while you are still on this earth? What purpose is there for your life? How does one benefit from being a Christian while still living in this world? How is a Christian able to deal with the challenges of life any differently than someone who does not know the Lord?

We cannot live in this world and find our purpose with our own human effort. Nor can we accomplish the tasks and assignments that will be required of us on our own. We cannot be righteous simply because we want to be. To identify and fulfill your purpose is a process; it requires a spiritual journey. To get there, you will need Jesus and His Holy Spirit to guide you along the way.

## BORN OF HIS SPIRIT

A new life in Jesus Christ and being born of His Spirit is the only "way" to Heaven, the only way to our Heavenly Father. Jesus said, "I am the WAY, the TRUTH, and the LIFE: no man comes to the Father, but by Me" (John 14:6).

Jesus is the WAY. Jesus is the only way to Heaven, the only path to Heaven. No one comes to the Father except through receiving Jesus Christ as Savior. The sin of Adam has passed through the blood of man over the ages and is within every human. It is the sin of Adam that separated man from God. It is the sin of Adam that causes man to sin and rebel against God. In the Old Testament, men sacrificed doves, sheep, lamb, and goats to atone for their sin. A blood sacrifice was required. However, they would sin, repeatedly, and then sacrifice again because the sacrifice did not enable or empower them to stop sinning.

Being born of Jesus' Spirit gives us a new beginning; we become born again. We no longer need to sacrifice to atone for our sin, as they did in the Old Testament. Jesus is the atonement (payment) for our sins. Being born again gives us access to God by His Holy Spirit who strengthens us to live righteously and holy. Being born again makes us His child, a child of the Most-High God and a sibling to our Savior! As God's child, like Jesus, we become heir to the Throne of Grace! We are so wretched in our natural self, our Holy God cannot even look at us, except through the filter of the blood of Jesus Christ, His Son. That is why every time we pray or speak to God, we must approach Him "in the Name of Jesus."

"Jesus is the TRUTH" (John 14:6). "And the Word became flesh, and dwelt among us ... full of grace and truth" (John 1:14). There's a major difference between truth and facts. The world is full of information, facts, and data, most of which is important, and some of which we all use daily. However, facts change; they are not forever. The value of your home today is not what it was 10 years ago, neither is your age or your weight. What was a fact yesterday is no longer a fact today. Information becomes irrelevant or obsolete, replaced with new information. Data is good for limited periods until it is replaced with new data. Christians are to base our lives on Truth, not information, facts, and data. Truth is always true. Truth is the Word of God, which is the same yesterday, today, and forever. "For the law was given through Moses, but grace and truth came through Jesus Christ" (John 1:17). "God's Word is Truth" (John 17:17). "God is Spirit, and those who worship Him must worship Him in spirit and truth" (John 4:24). When others say you are worthless, the Truth says you are "fearfully and wonderfully made" (Ps. 139:14). When others give up on you and forsake you, Truth says, "I will never leave you nor forsake you" (Heb. 13:5). In all that you say and do, keep your eyes and your heart on the Word of God, the Truth. "Ye shall know the truth, and the truth shall make you free" (John 8:32).

"Jesus is the LIFE" (John 14:6). Before Christ, we were simply existing, going about our daily lives almost robotically with no sense of real purpose or meaning for our lives. Receiving Jesus as our Savior is the beginning of our spiritual life and the beginning of really living. When we receive Jesus as our Savior, we are born again into a new life in Christ. When we receive Jesus, our spirit man comes alive, our spirit becomes connected with Jesus' Holy Spirit, and we have real life. "Therefore, if anyone is in Christ, he is a new creation; old things have passed away; behold all things have become new" (2 Cor. 5:17 NKJV). In Christ, we have a new start, a new beginning!

"God has dealt to every man the measure of faith" (Rom. 12:3) to believe that Jesus Christ is Lord. God has given each of us the opportunity to be saved. He has given every person on earth enough faith to receive Jesus as Lord, if, when presented with the Word, they desire to be saved, and if they choose to be saved. The Lord is "not willing that any should perish, but that all should come to repentance" (2 Pet. 3:9). Though God desires that all be saved, He allows us free will; He does not force His Will upon any man. He allows us to decide which way we will choose. "I have set before you life and death, blessing and cursing: therefore choose life, that both you and your descendants may live" (Deut. 30:19 NKJV). God tells us to "choose life," but He leaves the choice to us. Those who choose not to believe in Christ are condemned. "He who believes in Him is not condemned; but he who does not believe is condemned already, because he has not believed in the name of the only begotten Son of God. And this is the condemnation, that light has come into the world, and men loved darkness rather than light, because their deeds were evil. For everyone practicing evil hates the light, and does not come to the light, lest his deeds should be exposed. But he who does the truth comes to the light, that his deeds may be clearly seen, that they have been done of God" (John 3:18–21 NKJV).

Receiving Jesus Christ as your personal Lord and Savior is as easy as saying a few simple words that you believe in your heart. Say, "I believe that Jesus is the Son of God; that Jesus was crucified, died, and was buried; that Jesus rose from the dead and now sits in Heaven at the right hand of God. Jesus, come into my heart and save me from sin. I receive you in my heart as my personal Lord and Savior. Thank you for saving my soul." It is a marvelous thing to accept Jesus Christ as your Savior and to be born again and born of His Spirit. When we are saved, we are forgiven! We are justified! "Just-if-I'd" never sinned. We are free from indwelling sin. No matter what we have done in the past, God has forgiven us. There is no condemnation. "There is therefore now no condemnation to those who are in Christ Jesus, who do not walk according to the flesh, but according to the Spirit" (Rom. 8:1 NKJV).

Salvation is the first step. It is a great start, but we cannot stop there. Once saved, when we die, we will go to Heaven, and that is a glorious thing. However, God has greater plans for us. He wants us to receive the benefits of salvation while we are still living here on earth. Those who stop at salvation later wonder why they keep backsliding and why they continue to do the same old things they did before salvation. The answer? We must move beyond salvation, move on to the next level of spiritual maturity. Salvation gives us access to God. Along with salvation, we need to maximize our access to God by being empowered with

His Holy Spirit. The power of the Holy Spirit "in" you will enable you to carry out the deeds the Lord asks of you.

## FILLED WITH HIS SPIRIT

Salvation means we are born of His Spirit, but if we stop at salvation, we are yet not spiritually mature, and we will remain "babes in Christ" (1 Cor. 3). Just as newborn babies are helpless and totally dependent on the love, care, and provision of someone else, so is the case with babes in Christ; babes can do nothing for God. To maximize access to God and to grow to full spiritual maturity, we must also be filled with Jesus' Spirit, and then led by His Spirit.

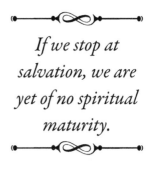

*If we stop at salvation, we are yet of no spiritual maturity.*

When we go beyond salvation and are filled with the Holy Spirit, we can develop a personal relationship with the Lord. We become God's living vessel on earth — a vessel in which He can dwell. Being God's living vessel is critical because "God is a Spirit, and those who worship Him must worship Him in Spirit and in Truth" (John 4:24). The whole reason God the Father wrapped God the Son in flesh and sent Jesus to the earth to die for us was that God knew the only way for man to overcome the sin of Adam and to obey God was for God Himself to live inside man and to strengthen man to resist the devil. Jesus came to die. He sacrificed His life so we could have His Holy Spirit living in us to empower us against sin. We become God's living vessel by receiving the indwelling power of His Holy Spirit living on the inside of us. The Holy Spirit is a **gift** from God, which He wants us to have, and which He freely gives us. All we must do is ask. "If ye then, being evil, know how to give good gifts unto your children: how much more will your Heavenly Father give the Holy Spirit to those who ask Him?" (Luke 11:13). Ask the Lord to fill you with His blessed Holy Spirit. He will.

Christians need the indwelling power of the Holy Spirit because we have an adversary, the devil. The adversary will continuously try to distract you from what the Lord wants you to do. He will routinely present you with temptations and beguiling offers. No one is strong enough in his own natural effort to resist the devil. The Bible tells us to "abstain from fleshly lusts, which war against the soul" (1 Pet. 2:11). Yes, even your flesh is an enemy to your soul, for "in your flesh dwelleth no good thing" (Rom. 7:18). Your flesh still has the sin nature of Adam. You need the power of the Holy Spirit **in** you to empower you to stand against the wiles of the devil and to stand against the lusts of your flesh. The indwelling power of Jesus' Holy Spirit living **in** you empowers you to live in this world but not to follow the ways of this world. The Holy Spirit in you enables you to have peace amid the storm; when trouble is on every side, you can have inner peace. The Holy Spirit in you will help you to stop backsliding, to resist the temptations of the devil, and to obey the Lord.

> *The Power of the Holy Spirit in you will enable you to carry out the deeds the Lord asks of you.*

God sacrificed His Son on the cross so that we would be able to have God Himself, through His Holy Spirit, empower us from within. "I will put my Spirit within you, and cause you to walk in my statutes, and ye shall keep my judgements, and do them" (Ez. 36:27). Once saved, you can have the Holy Spirit, the same power that raised Jesus from the dead, living <u>IN</u> you! It is the Holy Spirit IN you who will empower you to resist the temptations of this world. "And if Christ be in you, the body is dead because of sin; but the Spirit is life because of righteousness" (Rom. 8:10). Jesus came to die so that your spirit would have dominion over your flesh. The Holy Spirit in you is your Enabler;

He will enable you to do the work and to carry out the assignments the Lord gives to you. The Holy Spirit in you is your Comforter; He will comfort you in times of difficulty or distress. The Holy Spirit is your Director; He will direct you in what to do to carry out His assignment for your life. He will guide you during trials and tribulations, through every step of your journey. "I will not leave you comfortless: I will come to you" (John 14:18). **You cannot carry out the work of the Lord without the indwelling power of His blessed Holy Spirit.**

Only the Spirit knows the Spirit. Until we are born again and filled with Jesus' Spirit, we see not, understand not, and know not the things of the Spirit of God. The natural mind wants to think logically, scientifically, or intellectually, which is not according to the Word; it is worldly. "God is a Spirit and those who worship Him must worship Him in spirit and in truth" (John 4:24). We do not see, know or understand the things the Holy Spirit reveals to man, with our natural mind. We must look at everything from a spiritual perspective — from God's perspective. When you are filled with the Holy Spirit and look at things from a spiritual perspective, you will SEE what you are looking at. You will see when a person, situation, or choice is not right for you. Everything we say and everything we do in the natural, God sees in the Spirit. Everything we say and everything we do in the natural, we will please or displease, God.

## YOUR PRAYER LANGUAGE

Another gift God gives us, which comes with the indwelling of His Holy Spirit, is the gift of our own private prayer language, or what we call speaking in tongues. When we are filled with His Spirit, we can ask the Holy Spirit to pray for us, and pray through us, those things that need to be prayed. Often, we are not aware of the problems and challenges ahead of us. We may not know that our relative is having a health challenge or needs financial support. We may not know that our spouse will soon be terminated from work. We may not know that our teenager has been hanging around drug users. The Holy Spirit, God in us, knows what the problems are and what problems are coming. He knows the solutions, too. God loves us so much that He gives us His Holy Spirit to live in us and be our Enabler and our Guide. Whenever we call on the Holy Spirit to pray through us, He will. We just open our mouths and allow sound to come out. That sound will be different for each of us because God gives each of us our own private prayer language. "And they were all filled with the Holy Ghost, and began to speak with other tongues, as the Spirit gave them utterance" (Acts 2:4). The Holy Spirit prays for us when we don't know what or how to pray.

There are several key benefits to you praying in the spirit (speaking in tongues), a few of which include:

- "...he that speaketh in an unknown tongue speaketh not unto men, but unto God..." (I Cor. 14:2).
- "He that speaketh in an unknown tongue edifieth himself..." (edifieth himself: enlightens himself, educates himself, improves himself) (I Cor. 14:4)
- "...the Spirit Himself makes intercession on your behalf with groanings which cannot be understood" (Rom. 8:26).

When we first try to pray in the Spirit, our prayer language will sound like gibberish, because it is indeed another language. Your first words may sound like *rho be lah com tala*. Or, it could sound like *so de ca pour shi pe*. Remember, it is not you who is praying; "The Spirit Himself makes intercession on your behalf with groanings which cannot be understood" (Rom. 8:26). Regardless of what comes out or how it sounds, keep praying. Remember, it is you giving the Holy Spirit permission to pray through you. Also remember that your prayer language will not be in your native tongue. For example, if you speak English, your prayer language will not be in English. As it is with learning any other language, the more you speak it, the more fluent you will become. You will become fluent in your prayer language by frequently praying in the Spirit, so pray in the Spirit daily. Remember, this is your own private prayer language between you and the Lord. It is you giving the Lord permission, through the Holy Spirit, to pray for you, and through you, the things you do not know need to be prayed.

Often, we do not know what to pray for, but the Lord knows. Allow Him to pray through you for those things you may not even be aware of.

**Prayer for the Holy Spirit to Pray for Me and Through Me**
Dear Heavenly Father, I come to You in the name of my Lord and
Savior, Jesus Christ
Your Son, my Savior and my soon-coming King.
Thank you for Jesus.
Thank you for saving my soul.
Thank you, Jesus, for accepting your assignment.
Thank you for finishing your course.
Thank you that you are still seated at the right hand of God, Our
Father, making intercession on my behalf.
Jesus, thank you for keeping your promise to send your blessed
Holy Spirit.
Heavenly Father, in the name of Jesus, I ask You to fill me with your
blessed Holy Spirit
Let your anointing fall fresh on me.
Holy Spirit, I welcome you. Pray those things for me and through me
that I know not what I ought to pray.
Heavenly Father, I ask that you give me the interpretation of that
which your Spirit prays,
that it be profitable to my natural mind.
In Jesus' name, I pray.
[Pray in the Spirit]

Notice that this prayer includes asking the Lord to give you the interpretation of your prayer language, so you understand what you have prayed. You will likely not hear a direct interpretation. You may receive a knowing that an issue is taken care of, or you may sense that someone heavy on your heart needs to hear from you, or you need to take a specific action as the next step in your assignment. Always ask the Lord to give you an interpretation of that which the Holy Spirit prays through you. Listen, perceive, be sensitive to what He points out to you. What is He having you see, know, or do? Whatever He shows you, act on it, promptly.

## LED BY HIS SPIRIT

Once you accept Jesus as Savior, you must also accept Jesus as your Lord. This is an intentional decision to submit your will to the Will of God. Accepting Jesus as Lord is your choice for God's Will to be done in every area of your life. Submission of your will to the Will of your Heavenly Father is the acknowledgment that He knows what is best for you and that He is Lord of your life, not yourself.

We are pilgrims in this world, traveling through a distant land. We are visitors here. Being led by God's Spirit is necessary for every believer because we are in this world, but we are not of this world. God is our Father, and Heaven is our home. Our goal, as Christians, is to make it back home to our Father in Heaven. First, we must live our lives here on earth, fulfilling the purpose for which our Heavenly Father ordained for us since birth. The Lord sent us here with a purpose. To fulfill our purpose and make it back home to our Heavenly Father, we need a guide to show us the way.

Jesus IS the WAY. Jesus left us His Holy Spirit to be our guide. The Holy Spirit will lead us daily in the way we should go. He will lead us in our decisions, our choices, our actions, our activities, and our relationships *if* we allow Him.

Scripture tells us, "In all thy ways acknowledge Him, and He shall direct thy paths" (Prov. 3:6). This verse says in *all* thy ways — not just the big stuff, the crises, and the severe challenges. *All* includes the big things, the medium things, and even the little stuff.

Ask the Lord to lead you through the indwelling power of His Holy Spirit in everything you do. As you go through your day, continuously ask, "What would you have me do about this, Lord? Show me what you want me to see." The Word tells us to "pray without ceasing" (1 Thess. 5:17), which is accomplished by continuously asking the Lord to lead you, to show you, and to empower you as you give thanks and praise for Him doing so.

Before you make that important business call, ask the Lord to guide your mind and your thoughts and to give you the words to say. Ask Him to go before you and to touch the heart of the person you are calling that they be open and receptive to your plight. The Lord knows what the other person needs, and needs to hear, so ALLOW the Lord to use you to speak to the person and manifest His Will.

When you ask the Lord to lead you, ALLOW Him to lead. You must *allow* Him to lead, because being led by the Holy Spirit requires a conscious, submissive decision on your part to accept and walk as He leads, guides, and directs. This is the most challenging, yet one of the most rewarding, phases of spiritual growth. It is challenging, because often, what the Lord leads you to do will NOT make sense to your natural mind. Your flesh (carnal nature) never wants to obey God. Your carnal man will want to do its own thing and make its own decision. After all, you are smart, you are intelligent, and you know how to make good decisions. Nonetheless, remember that no matter how smart or intelligent you are, you have thimble-sized knowledge compared to our omniscient, all-knowing Heavenly Father. It is rewarding because we have the assurance that God gives the best to those who leave the choice to Him. He will "never leave us or forsake us" (Heb. 13:5). "He will guide our feet into the way of peace" (Luke 1:79). Allow the Lord to lead you.

Consider this analogy as an example of how the Holy Spirit leads and guides us. In movies and TV shows where cops are in a high-speed chase going after the bad guys, there is one thing that is consistent in every chase: the helicopter. We always see the pilot in the helicopter telling the police on the ground something like, "He turned right on Crescent Road," or "He turned left into the alley between 4th and 5th Streets." The police on the ground rely on the helicopter pilot to guide them because on the ground, the view is restricted. The police on the ground must deal with traffic and their visibility is limited because of trucks, trees and tall buildings. On the other hand, the helicopter pilot has a bird's-eye view of the whole scene. He has clear visibility of every move the bad guy makes on the ground. The pilot with the bird's-eye view guides the police on the ground in every turn. The police on the ground depend on the pilot; they do not argue with the one who has the bird's-eye view. The police don't ignore the pilot and make their own decision to turn somewhere. The police on the ground follow instructions from the pilot who has the bird's-eye view; they turn where they are led to turn; they speed up when they are told to speed up, following the guidance precisely. The police on the ground know that if they follow the pilot's instructions, it will lead them to exactly where they need to go.

That is how you must be with the leading of the Holy Spirit. You are on the ground with a limited and restricted view. The Lord has a bird's-eye view of everything going on in your life. The Lord is omniscient; He knows everything. He knows what is around the corner in your life. He knows where your roadblocks are, where the potholes are, and where the bad people are. He knows what you have gone through, what is currently going on in your life, and what is coming. He wants to lead you in the WAY you should go. He wants to direct your path to lead you exactly to where you need to go, how you should go, and what you need to do to get there. He has plans for you there.

The Lord is omnipresent. God is already in your tomorrows, working things out on your behalf. That means He already knows what situations you will face and what challenges are ahead of you. The Lord is omnipotent; He IS power. He wants to empower you to handle each challenge. He will strengthen you and lead you through today's challenges; some will be delightful, and others will be tough, but they will prepare you for tomorrow's challenges. Whatever the challenges may be or how difficult they may become God will give you the grace to make it through to the end. Grace is the omnipotent power of God working in you for the glory of God. Your Heavenly Father will give you grace to carry out tasks He wants of you that you could never accomplish on your own. The Lord will do the work through you. "Grace and truth came by Jesus Christ" (John 1:17). Jesus loves you; He will never mislead you. The Lord will always guide you in the way you should go. And, HE is always right! By an act of your own will, submit your will to the Lord's Will. Follow His lead.

For me, being led by the Lord is the next best thing to salvation. I LOVE to be led by the Holy Spirit. I find it exciting and even exhilarating at times. It is always an adventure. You may have heard of the movie character Crocodile Dundee — the guy with all the adventures. Well, I say, "Crocodile Dundee ain't got nothing on me! I've got my own adventure going on!" Why is it an adventure? Because you never know what the Lord is going to tell you to do. You never know how it is going to turn out. You just learn that obedience brings the reward. You learn through His faithfulness to you that it will always turn out for your good and for the benefit of others. It is fresh and exciting every day. It is the most rewarding experience ever!

People who play video games are operating in a virtual world; they push buttons to play with fictional characters who have pretend powers. Being led by the Holy Spirit puts you in the real game; it is the game of life in the real world on a spiritual realm, using supernatural powers of the Holy Spirit to overcome every obstacle the enemy throws your way. The supernatural power of the Holy Spirit brings you a holy boldness and a blessed assurance, knowing that, with the power of the Lord operating in you, through you, and for you, you can do all things, You already have the victory. Now, that's an adventure!

## MEMBER OF THE BODY OF CHRIST

Being born of His Spirit, filled with His Spirit, and led by His Spirit are essential to carrying out the Will of the Father. Church membership is also essential. You must become a member of a Bible-believing, Bible-teaching church. The church represents the Body of Christ. As a member of the church, you become a part of that Body. Just as the natural body has parts that function to carry out tasks and assignments, so does the Body of Christ. As a member of the church, you become a functioning part of the Body of Christ. As part of the Body, the Lord can then use you to carry out tasks and assignments that are of His Will. The Lord will use you to bless others in the Body, and He will use others in the Body to bless you. That is why you must not only become a member of the Body, but regular church attendance is also essential. Scripture tells us to "forsake not the assembling of ourselves together" (Heb. 10:25).

The Lord uses pastors and ministers in churches to teach members about the ways of the Lord, how to stay holy, how to walk by faith, why we should not continually ask God for "stuff," how to please God, and more. The Holy Spirit speaks to the pastor during the preparation of the message and leads the pastor in how to minister to the needs of the members. When you are a regular participating member, you will hear your need addressed by the pastor. You will hear guidance and instruction on how to handle your personal situation. The message may be so personal to you that you may often wonder if the pastor was eavesdropping in your house. The pastor will not call you by name from the pulpit, but you will discern that the message pertained especially to you. This is what happens when the Holy Spirit, who knows your needs, speaks to the pastor during the preparation of the message, and ministers to the pastor about the needs of the people. Members hear the message according to what their unique needs are. They receive guidance, comfort, or instruction in line with what is going on in their life. Even when members feel chastised by the message, it is the Lord correcting them and preparing them toward being the person, and doing the work, the Lord desires of them. Therefore, church membership and regular attendance are biblical requirements.

Once you join the church and are attending regularly, you must also get involved in the life of the church. This means participating in a ministry within the church. Serving in a ministry is the very best way to get to know the church and other members. Serving in a ministry is also the place where the Lord will begin to strengthen you. As you interact with other members, situations and challenges will arise that present opportunities to demonstrate that you have learned and are living out the messages taught by the pastor. Whether the situations are encouraging or challenging, they represent opportunities for you to demonstrate your spiritual growth. Opportunities such as these will also present themselves on your job, in your community, and in your home. They will serve as tests of your character and tests of your spiritual maturity.

As a child of God, growing, maturing, and learning is an ongoing, never-ending process. Serving in a Bible-believing, Bible-teaching church will teach you, mature you, and strengthen your spiritual walk.

*Chapter 2*

# ESTABLISH A RELATIONSHIP
# WITH THE LORD

When you meet someone new whom you find interesting, you spend time talking with that person. You want to know all about them, and you want them to know about you. You spend time with them. You ask questions. You share your thoughts, hopes, and plans. You want to hear what they think about you and your plans. You want to hear their hopes and plans. You want to tell them what you think about them. You want them to be a part of your plans, to support you in your work. You want them to be with you through good times and difficult times. You need to know that you can depend on them, and you want them to know that they can depend on you.

Establish a personal relationship with the Lord the same as you established a relationship with the person you found interesting:

- Talk with Him regularly
- Thank Him for Jesus and for saving your soul
- Thank Him for providing for you and your family
- Read His Word, the Bible, daily
- Ask questions
    - What would He have you do about a situation?

- o How to do something you've not done before
- o When you're puzzled about a situation, ask Him to show you what is going on
- Ask Him to show you what you are doing that you need to stop doing
- Ask Him to show you what you are not doing that you need to start doing
- Ask Him to show you things about yourself that please Him, and displease Him, and how to fix it
- Ask Him to show you people, places and things currently in your life that are not good for you
  - o Ask Him to remove them from your life, and then give them up
  - o Ask Him to surround you with godly people
- Ask Him for wisdom and understanding
- Thank Him for Jesus, for saving your soul; thank Jesus for sacrificing His life for you
  - o Thank Him for keeping His promise to send His Holy Spirit
  - o Ask Him to fill you afresh with His anointing, to let His Holy Spirit fall fresh on you
  - o Ask Him to fill you with His blessed Holy Spirit
  - o Ask Him to lead, guide and direct you
  - o Ask Him to pray through you in your private prayer language, and then pray in the Spirit
- Ask Him to give you a pure heart, to search your heart and remove anything that does not please Him
- Praise Him for being God, and God all by Himself
- Worship Him for being your omniscient, omnipresent and omnipotent Father
- Thank Him for His unconditional love for you

- o His loving-kindness, His tender mercies, His grace, His favor
- o His protection, His provision for you
- o His forgiveness
- Keep your commitments to Him
- Be a credible witness
- Obey Him and what He leads you to do
- Trust Him with everything
- Love Him

I thought I loved the Lord since I had been going to church all my life. But even though I had grown up in the church, I was in my early twenties before I realized I needed to know the Lord for myself and have a personal relationship with Him. I learned that you can't love Him until you get to know Him, just like any other relationship.

I also learned that loving the Lord is something that you must WANT to do. We love Him only as much as we obey Him. Obeying the Lord is a choice! Our natural inclination is to do things our way and to do things we want to do, even when we say we are serving the Lord. We naturally lean on our own understanding and resist the voice of the Lord. The resisting may not even be obvious to you; you may simply think there is an easier way to do something, or you may not know how to accomplish something the Lord says. In either case, leaning on your own understanding is operating in pride, stubbornness, and rebellion. "The Lord resists the proud, and gives Grace to the humble" (1 Pet. 5:5). Pride, stubbornness and rebellion are not of God, and they thwart any faint attempts to please God. Further, "the Lord sees stubbornness as idolatry and rebellion as witchcraft" (1 Sam. 15:23). When we lean to our own understanding rather than follow the Lord, we are being prideful, stubborn and self-reliant. God resists the proud, and sees stubbornness as idolatry. When we refuse to do what God says we are rebelling against God. In His eyes, we are practicing idolatry and witchcraft. Remember, we love Him only as much as we obey Him.

The Lord loves us unconditionally. He loves us enough that He sacrificed His Son to die for us. Now the Lord wants us to love Him. "The LORD our God is one LORD: and thou shalt love the LORD thy God with all thine heart, and with all thy soul, and with all thy might" (Deut. 6:4–5). Learning to love the Lord is a process. The more you talk to Him and share your thoughts, the more you will feel comfortable in talking with Him. The more you ask Him for guidance and strength, the more you will feel reassured of His love for you. The more you obey Him, the more rewarding you will feel. The more you develop a relationship with Him, the more you will trust Him and see His unconditional love for you. You will see His grace and mercy toward you. All of this will cause you to fall in love with Him.

## DEVELOP YOUR PRAYER LIFE

Daily devotion, a set-aside time for prayer and communion with the Lord, feeds and nourishes your spirit. Just as we feed our flesh every day for strength, we must also feed and strengthen our spirit daily. We need the Lord to lead us, protect us, provide for us, give us peace, comfort us... We need a lot from the Lord, every day, and He is there for us every day. Make a point to set aside time every day just to devote to Him, no matter how busy you may be. The busier you are, the more you need Him. Have a daily time of devotion; a time set aside just to pray, thank, praise, and worship the Lord. Daily devotion is the key to your spiritual growth and natural success.

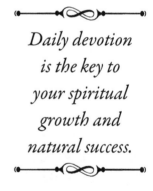

*Daily devotion is the key to your spiritual growth and natural success.*

Pray in ways that are right for you, according to the Word of God. No need to be fancy or formal with your prayer; just be real. God knows you. He knows how you think, how you talk, how you express yourself. Talk with the Lord as if He is the perfect daddy, who loves you, protects you, provides for you, always has your back, and loves you unconditionally.

I have included a few of my prayers as examples. However, these are my prayers. Use them if you choose. Modify them if you want. Use parts, delete parts, or create your own. The key is to pray.

## Prayer of Thanksgiving

Every prayer should be a prayer of thanksgiving. We should never go to God for anything without thanking Him first. We all have so much to be thankful for; we should start each prayer thanking the Lord for something. Thank Him for Jesus and for saving your soul. Thank Him for His grace, His mercy, His ever-loving kindness, His Holy Spirit, His protection, His provision, and His Love. Thank Him for health and family; the list is endless. No matter what it is that you may want or need, start with thanking the Lord for what He has already done for you, in you, and in your life.

The first thing you should ask for is forgiveness. Yes, Jesus has already saved us, forgiven us, and justified us, but we sin every day in some form or another. It could be a thought of something we want or don't want; our attitude towards something or someone; not helping when it was within our power to do; not forgiving someone; or failing to obey that still, quiet voice. Forgiveness gives us a clean slate to write our prayer requests to the Lord.

Prayer of Praise and Thanksgiving

Dear Heavenly Father, in the name of Jesus, I come to you as your child, asking you to forgive me of my every thought, word, deed and inaction that does not please you. Thank you for being my loving and forgiving Father. Thank you for who you are, and for who you are in my life. You are my rock, my sword, my shield, my buckler, my strong tower, my ever-present help in the time of trouble. You are my hiding place, my shelter from the storm, and my shadow from the heat. You are the light unto my path, and the lamp unto my feet. You are the God who healeth me. Thank you, Jesus, that by your stripes I am healed. Thank you that your Word is medicine to my flesh and marrow to my bones. Thank you for saving my soul. Thank you for calling me to be your child. Thank you for growing me up into you. Thank you for purging, pruning, and perfecting me. Thank you for maturing me. Thank you that I can do all things through Christ who strengthens me. Bless that I be a creditable witness for you, Lord, seen and read by all men. Bless me to speak your Word, and use your Word, in every situation and in every conversation.

In Jesus' name, I pray. Amen.

Pray for guidance and direction in everything you do and plan to do. Ask the Lord to lead you in what to do, when to do it, how to do it, and with whom to work.

Pray for others. Praying for others matures you, strengthens you, gives you peace, and keeps your heart pure. Pray for those who mistreat you. Pray for those who are lost, sick, alone, poor, angry, violent, depressed, hungry, motherless, and fatherless. Pray for families, youth, men, women, children, and communities. Pray for our nation and our leaders. Above all, pray that God's Will be done.

Prayer of Grace for our Food

Dear Heavenly Father, thank you for the food I am about to receive. Please sanctify this food, removing anything from it that would do me any harm. Bless that this food provides the healing nutrition my body needs to be strong, vibrant and healthy. Bless that I use the energy from this food to go forward and do Your Will and do it Your way.

In Jesus' name, I pray. Amen.

Prayer of Worship

Dear Heavenly Father, you are Lord God Jehovah, the self-sustaining God. You are God, and God all by yourself. When you want counsel, you look within and you counsel yourself, because you are **omniscient;** you know everything. You know me, Lord. In the crevices of my soul, you know me. In the inner chambers of my heart, you know me. In the secret thoughts of my mind, you know me. Yet, you love me anyway.

You are **omnipresent;** you were with me before you placed me in my mother's womb, and you've been with me all these many years. You are already in my tomorrows, working things out on my behalf. You've already been in today and have set the course for my day. I submit my will to your Will for today and every day. Thy Will be done. Thy Will alone be done in me, with me, by me, for me, to me, and through me, to your glory and to your honor.

You are **omnipotent.** You are power, and all power is yours. You have the power to do all things and to make them come to past. You have the power to enable me to do the things you have called me to do. I submit myself to you, Heavenly Father, and I submit to your plans for me. In the name of Jesus, I go forth boldly to do your Will and to do it your way, such that you be glorified, and all who see or hear me to be edified, to your glory and your honor.

In Jesus' name, I pray. Amen.

When you have a need, ask the Lord for wisdom and guidance. Yes, wisdom and guidance on addressing your need. Never pray for tangible things that you can work for, earn money, and purchase. Rather than asking God for a car, house, vacation, or anything that you can buy with money, pray for wisdom and guidance for whatever the need may be.

For example, when my mortgage fell behind, I prayed and asked the Lord to show me the best way to bring it current. When my car became too old to rely on anymore, I prayed and asked the Lord to direct me in what do to about transportation.

The car I had been driving was my dream car. I sacrificed until I could purchase it and went to the showroom, selected exactly what I wanted, and drove it home. I loved that car. It fit me perfectly. It was a perfect reflection of my personality, style, and profession. I drove that car for 12 years. I drove that car for seven years *after* the note was paid off. By then, my financial situation had changed, and I did not want to take on another new car note. My beautiful car-baby was now old and wearing out. I knew it was no longer strong enough for me to rely on as my only vehicle.

The Scripture tells us, "In all thy ways acknowledge Him, and He will direct your path" (Prov. 3:6). *Acknowledge* Him means to ask Him, and He will lead you in what to do. However, the "ask" is not for stuff you can buy; the ask is for wisdom and guidance. In every area of our life, everything we do, the Lord wants us to come to Him and to ask Him what to do.

### Prayer for Direction

Dear Heavenly Father, in the name of Jesus, I thank you for Jesus. Thank you, Jesus, for accepting your assignment. Thank you for finishing your course. Thank you for sitting at the right hand of God, OUR Father, making intercession on my behalf. Thank you for keeping your promise to send your blessed Holy Spirit. Holy Spirit, I offer myself to you as an empty and open vessel for you to use as you choose. Fill me afresh, Heavenly Father; let Your anointing fall fresh on me. Lord, thy Will be done, and thy Will alone be done in me, with me, by me, for me, to me, and through me in Jesus' name. Order my steps, Lord Jesus. Guide me in the way I should go. Guide my mind, my thoughts, my words, my actions, my reactions, my perceptions, my demeanor, my countenance, my body language, my attitude, and my emotions, so that I might be a credible witness to all who see or hear me, so that all I say and all that I do will bless and glorify your holy name.

In Jesus' name, I pray. Amen

I asked the Lord what I should do about a car. I recognized that I would not be able to rely on my car-baby much longer, and He knew I did not want to take on a new car note. In my profession, I would frequently transport clients, so I asked the Lord to show me what to do for a car that would be nice enough to transport my clients, still without having a new car note. I pondered this with the Lord for a couple months. I never went shopping for a car.

One day, I was driving my car-baby, and I had my little dog, Milo, with me in the car. Milo is a 12-pound Bichon Frieze that was a gift to me from a business colleague. As I was driving, Milo needed to go potty. I drove past a strip mall looking for a nice patch of grass to stop and let Milo relieve himself. The grass did not look good at that mall, so I drove to another. The grass did not look good there either, so I drove to another; then another, then another. Then I thought, why in the world am I driving strip mall to strip mall, just to let this dog pee? I got to the fifth strip mall, spotted a beautiful plot of grass, and let Milo out so he could finally relieve himself.

As I was pulling out of the parking lot, I spotted a car that was also pulling out. The car started flashing at me. (Well, the car did not actually flash at me. When the Lord wants my attention on a certain thing, that thing will flash in my sight. The same thing happens with Scripture.) When the car started flashing, I also noticed that it had a for sale sign in the window. The car pulled out, and I had to wait for traffic before I could pull out.

As the Lord would have it, the car stopped at the light. The space beside it "just happened" to be empty, so I pulled to the lane along-side the car. The lane "just happened" to be on the side where the for-sale sign was on the window. I wrote down the number. The car was nothing like my car-baby. The car was a type of car that I had never considered purchasing; but the car flashed at me, so I knew I was to follow through.

When I got home, I called to inquire about the car. The seller lived only three miles from me, so I went to check the car out. It had only 23,000 miles on it and was garage kept. The owner and his wife had four cars and just did not need to keep this one. I test-drove the car; it was practically like new. The seller wanted only $19,000 for the car. It was a Mercedes Benz, CLK 350 with 23,000 miles. I knew the Lord selected this car just for me to purchase. I never saw myself as a Benz person; my car-baby was a Lexus. The seller asked if two weeks would be long enough for me to get my financing together. I told him yes and gave him a security deposit of $100.00.

I went home and did nothing about the car. I did not contact my credit union about financing. I was not anxious about the car. Two weeks later, the seller phoned me and asked if I were still interested in the car, and if I had gotten my financing. I told him I was still interested and then got on the phone to secure the financing. I had someone drop me off at the seller's house. I paid for the car and the seller followed me to my home as I drove the Benz. Once we got to my home, the seller took his tags off the car.

The Benz sat in my driveway for a solid month with no tags. I, again, was not anxious about the car. Frankly, I wanted to be sure it was not my "flesh" that wanted this car. Many people make a big deal about a Benz. I was thankful for the car, for sure, because I knew the Lord orchestrated for me to get that particular car. I simply wanted to be sure my flesh, or wanting to "be seen," was not an underlying motivation for getting the car. A month passed with the car sitting in my driveway with no tags. By then, I felt comfortable that it was not my flesh wanting the car, but simply a blessing from the Lord. I got all the papers in order and submitted them to the DMV. I had a beautiful, fairly new vehicle that was totally appropriate to transport my clients, and I did not take on the weight of a new car note. I was thankful and exceedingly grateful.

The Lord will indeed direct our path when we ask Him to guide us in what to do. I had asked the Lord what to do about getting another car, and He led me through the entire process, starting the day when I drove strip mall to strip mall finding a place so Milo could finally relieve himself on good grass. What the Lord was doing was

*The Lord gives the best to those who leave the choice to Him.*

orchestrating all things to come together for me to get THAT car. He was prodding me to go further down the road to that fifth strip mall because He knew that is where the seller of that car would be, that day, and at that time. The Lord orchestrated me getting THAT car. When God orchestrates, He orchestrates! When you pray, do not tell the

Lord to give you a specific thing. The Lord gives the best to those who leave the choice to Him.

## Come Boldly to the Throne

Several years ago, I heard someone pray. It was someone I knew well, and I knew they loved the Lord. They were leading a small group in prayer and said, "Father, you said to come boldly to the throne, so I come boldly to you and I **demand** that you <u>do this</u>, and I **demand** that you <u>do that</u>." Right at that moment, my heart grieved terribly for them. I knew them well enough that I knew they loved the Lord. I knew they meant no harm or disrespect to the Lord. I knew they were earnestly petitioning the Lord for a purpose. However, I recognized in that moment that they had been grossly mis-taught in what it meant to come boldly to the throne.

The Lord does want us to come boldly to Him. Boldly, meaning confidently, knowing that He loves us and cares for us. Boldly, meaning with a blessed assurance that He will hear us and answer us. Boldly, meaning as a child, meek and humble, trusting Him to give us what is best for us. We may not get what we ask for, just as a child asks for a giant lollipop but the parent, knowing it is not good for the child, gives what is best for the child. As Christians (Christ-like ones), we are to follow the example of Christ, who never demanded anything of the Father. Even in the Garden of Gethsemane, just before the crucifixion, Jesus prayed, "O my Father, if this cup may not pass away from me, except I drink it, Thy Will be done" (Matt. 26:42). Look at our earthly father. Do we demand anything of our daddies? Do we tell our natural father what we demand? No. This is sorely out of line with the Word of God.

The Word says, "Let us therefore come boldly unto the throne of grace, that we may obtain mercy, and find grace to help in time of need" (Heb. 4:16). God wants us to come boldly to Him with confidence that

He loves us, that He knows our need and will be merciful to help us, that He will give us the grace to make it through. When we go boldly to the Throne, we go as His child, confidently asking for guidance in our need, with a blessed assurance that He loves us, hears us, and will answer with mercy and grace for our need. The Lord always gives what is best for us.

## SEEK THE LORD, RESIST THE DEVIL

One of the main things the Lord wants from us is for us to seek Him, to seek His Kingdom, and to seek His righteousness. The Scripture tells us, "Seek the Lord while He may be found" (Is. 55:6). Seek means to search for, hunt for, look for, try to find, strive for. Seek Him daily, seek Him in every situation. Seek Him during the good times, the bad times, and the "everything is just fine" times.

The Word also tells us to "submit yourself therefore unto God. Resist the devil, and he will flee from you" (James 4:7). We must do all three: seek the Lord, submit to the Lord, and resist the devil.

<u>Seek the Lord</u>: The more we seek the Lord, the more we will submit to the Lord. Submitting to the Lord means inviting Him into your very being — into your thoughts, your actions, your words. It is asking the Lord to guide you at each decision. He tells us, "In all your ways acknowledge Him, and He shall direct your paths" (Prov. 3:6). To acknowledge Him, simply ask Him. Remember, when God says "all" thy ways, He means ALL thy ways: the big things and the small stuff. Seeking the Lord is asking Him questions about everything. What should I do about this? How should I handle that? What would you have me say to them? Why am I not moving forward in what you told me to do? How should I do this project? How should I handle this situation? Ask Him genuinely, and listen for His answer. The answer will come as a realization, a knowing in your heart, a blessed assurance as to what it is you must do.

Seeking the Lord is also thanking Him for everything: the big stuff and the little stuff. Thank Him for His grace, mercy, and His ever-loving kindness. Thank Him for Jesus, salvation, forgiveness, and His Holy Spirit. Thank Him when you almost fall but do not. Thank Him when you almost have an accident but do not. Thank Him when you hear your grown child tell their child something you instilled in them growing up. Thank Him when He provides a way to pay for a major repair when you had no idea how you would cover the cost. Thank Him for favor in your job. Thank Him when you pay your bills. Thank Him for peace in your home. Thank Him all day, every day, for everything.

Scripture says we should "pray without ceasing" (1 Thess. 5:16). When you are asking the Lord questions all day about everything you do, and thanking Him all day for everything He does or has done, you are praying without ceasing.

Submit to the Lord. Submit simply means to give in to God's Will. Surrender your will recognizing God's Will is always going to be what is best for you. Remember, He is omnipresent, He is already in your tomorrows working things out on your behalf. Submit your thoughts, your plans, your desires, yourself, your children; all that you are and hope to be – surrender to the Lord. Allow His Holy Spirit to lead, guide and direct you in all you say, think and do.

Rather than asking the Lord for material things, consider changing your approach. Ask Him for wisdom, understanding, discernment. Ask Him to give you a pure heart, and the mind of Christ. Ask Him to lead, guide and direct you in all you say and do.

Thank Him for being your loving Father. Tell Him that you love Him. Tell Him that you want to get to know Him (He already knows you). Tell Him that you want to establish a personal relationship with Him, and then make the commitment to do so. You may want to use the list of questions at the beginning of this chapter to strengthen your relationship with the Lord.

Resist the Devil. The Word tells us, "Resist the devil, and he will flee from you" (Jas. 4:7). Resisting the devil means to fight against or refuse to give in to his temptations. Newly saved Christians may still be "in the world." New Christians may still party and do the club routine, thinking that because they "got saved," they are ok. Not so. We must "come out from among them and be separate" (2 Cor. 6:17). As Christians, we are to be distinctively different from those who are still in the world. As Christians, we are in this world, but not of this world. We cannot do the same things that those who are unsaved do and think that it is alright with the Lord.

The devil is the adversary, your enemy. No matter what niceties he presents to you, his intent will always be to destroy you. The enemy will constantly try to entice you with the things you find pleasure doing. He will present you with people you find attractive, situations that look like opportunities, and material things that will be very enticing. That is what the devil does; he entices. He presents and persuades. The devil presents enticing things to you and tries to persuade you that it is good for you. Do not fall for his game.

Resisting the devil means resisting the temptation for the things that do not glorify the Lord: resisting the nightlife and fast times; resisting behaviors, people, habits, and addictions — everything that is contrary to the Word. Resist means to refuse to give in. Resist the devil and he will flee from you. Again, resist the devil and he will flee. If you stand strong in the Lord and in the power of His might, resisting the devil, the devil will get tired of tempting you, knowing you will just fight against him. Resist the devil and he will flee. That does not mean he will not try again later. It means resist every time the devil presents something to you and tries to persuade you toward something that is not of God.

People who are unsaved, and often new Christians who are still babes in Christ, do the opposite of what they should do; they seek the devil and resist the Lord! Your flesh may still want to hang on to that party life, that person you KNOW is no good for you, or that place you like to go to so you can kickback. Such activities are ways of the world and the opposite of what the Word says.

Think of it this way: The devil knows what you like, and he will continually present it to you as long as you let your "flesh" rule. That is why we need the indwelling power of the Holy Spirit in us to strengthen us to resist temptation. "Resist the devil, and he will flee" (Jas 4:7). How do you resist the devil? Resist temptations. The temptations do not necessarily have to be overtly sinful; they may be subtle but enticing. The more enticing something is, the more you must resist it.

No matter what the adversary presents to you, the Lord will strengthen you to resist if you seek Him and ask Him to strengthen you. "There is no temptation known to man that the Lord has not already made a way of escape for you" (1 Cor. 10:13). While you are being tempted, ask the Lord to help you. In the midst of feeling enticed, ask the Lord to strengthen you. "Your spirit is willing, but your flesh is weak" (Matt. 26:41). This means your spirit wants to please the Lord, but your natural inclination is to please yourself. You cannot resist the devil on your own strength. Earnestly ask the Lord to strengthen you right then during the temptation. The Lord will show you the way of escape from the temptation when you sincerely petition Him for help.

Make up your mind that you will no longer do the things that you know are against the Word of God. It is a simple decision that only you can make. You simply must make up your stubborn mind that you will choose to do God's Will and not your will. You will err every time doing your own will. You can never go wrong doing God's Will.

Your body has a mind of its own and wants what it wants. You are spirit made in the image of God. Because we live in this world, on this earth, we must live in a natural body. But YOU are spirit. Your spirit lives in a body. You are not your body; your body is just your house and transportation. Make your body obey the Word of God. Bring your flesh under subjection; deny your flesh anything that does not please

God. Make yourself obey the Word and the Will of the Lord. Align your will with God's Will. Ask the Lord to lead you and then follow as He leads.

## Promises with Conditions

The Lord has made many promises in His Word, and all His promises He keeps. However, when the promise comes with a condition, then the condition is something YOU must meet. There are things YOU must do, and conditions you must meet, to reap the benefits of the Lord's promises.

Scripture tells us to "seek first the Kingdom of God and His righteousness, and all these things shall be added unto you" (Matt. 6:33). However, notice that this Scripture is a promise, with a condition:

- The promise: All these things shall be added unto you.
- The condition: Seek first the Kingdom of God and His righteousness.

*The Lord has made many promises, and all His promises He will keep. When the promise has conditions, the condition is something YOU must meet.*

The Lord already KNOWS what we need. He's God! He is omniscient. He knows everything. He is Jehovah Jireh, our provider. Just as a good parent plans for the needs of their child, so does our Heavenly Father have plans of provision for us, His children. First, we must meet the condition to receive the promise. When we seek the Kingdom of God and His righteousness, the Lord will add unto us the things we need.

Most people focus solely on what they hope to receive from the promise; they totally overlook the condition. They overlook the action they must take before they can receive the promise. For many of us, our focus is entirely on what God promised He would do. We pray and pray, reminding God of His Word, reminding God of His promise. God hears us every time we pray, but until you meet the condition, it is YOU who is holding back the promise. Your failure to meet the condition is tying God's hand from blessing you with the promise.

Many of God's promises have conditions. Other examples of God's promises with conditions include the following:

1) "For if ye forgive men their trespasses, your heavenly Father will also forgive you" (Matt. 6:14).
   a. Promise: Your Heavenly Father will forgive your trespasses.
   b. Condition: Forgive men their trespasses.

2) "Judge not, and ye shall not be judged: condemn not, and ye shall not be condemned: forgive, and ye shall be forgiven" (Luke 6:37).
   a. Promise: God will not judge you or condemn you, and He will forgive you.
   b. Condition: Do not judge others or condemn others, and forgive others.

3) "What things so ever ye desire, when ye pray, believe that ye receive them, and ye shall have them" (Mark 11:24).
   a. Promise: Ye shall have what things you desire when you pray.
   b. Condition: Believe that you receive them.

   NOTE: Be careful. Do not "ask amiss" (foolishly or outside His Word). "Things" in this verse mean whatever questions you have of Him or whatever guidance you need. Ask, believing God will answer, and He will give it to you. "Things" does not refer to stuff you can buy or even stuff you can touch. Things are spiritual questions for guidance, direction, wisdom, and understanding.

4) "In all thy ways acknowledge Him, and He will direct your paths" (Prov. 3:6).
   a. Promise: God will direct your paths (note, paths is plural).
   b. Condition: In all your ways (everything you do) acknowledge Him (ask Him what to do and how to do it).

God delights in answering us and blessing us when we ask for things. However, "faith is the substance of things hoped for, the evidence of things NOT seen" (Heb. 11:1). Faith is the evidence of things not seen. Faith is for acquiring what we cannot see. Never waste your time asking God for things you can buy or things you can see; never ask for "stuff." Stuff is easy to acquire; just earn money and purchase it. God wants to give us spiritual things: answers, guidance, direction, wisdom. For example, ask the Lord for guidance and wisdom in how to acquire, or if you should acquire something. When my car-baby was on the fritz, I asked the Lord to show me what to do about getting another car, and He led me right to the exact next car. Ask Him what to do and how to do whatever it is, and He will guide you to the answer.

However, while you are working towards meeting the condition, be sure to keep your heart right before the Lord. Do not allow yourself to doubt, and do not get impatient. Continue to operate in faith as you work towards meeting the condition, believing that God sees, hears, and knows your concern. Continue to exercise patience. It may take a while for you to meet the condition. It may take even longer for you to receive the promise. You will inherit the promise through faith and patience. The Word tells us "be not slothful, but followers of them who through faith and patience inherit the promises" (Heb. 6:12).

## Claim Your Position

Every now and then, we can allow the situations, frustrations, and even people around us to weigh us down. We feel we are in the doldrums. We drag along, knowing something is wrong but not sure what may be the problem. Perhaps we are depressed. Sometimes we can even feel disconnected from God. There are numerous conditions that, if we allow them, they will get us down. The operative word here is **IF** we allow them. We know the Lord will never leave us or forsake us, so there must be something we need to do to get back on track.

*The only thing you have to fight with, and the only thing you need for the fight, is the Word of God.*

The adversary will constantly try to throw you off course, especially when you are making progress in your spiritual growth in the Lord. The adversary wants nothing more than to distract you from following the Lord. When this happens, you cannot rely on your flesh, your mind, or your feelings to get you back on course. The only thing you have to fight with, and the only thing you need for the fight, is the Word of God.

In times like this, YOU must take command of your flesh. You must snap back to reality, to the Truth of God's Word. Remind the devil who you are and whose you are. Claim your position in the Lord as a child of God.

Claim Your Position
in the Lord
*Stand on your feet!*

*(Boldly proclaim, in a loud and commanding voice:)*

I am a child of the Most-High God!
Heir to the Throne of Grace!
Sibling to my Savior!
No weapon formed against me shall prosper!
Thank You Lord that you bless whatsoever I set my hands to do
to prosper!
In the name of Jesus!

When this happens to me, I stand up and boldly proclaim in a loud and commanding voice: "I am a child of the Most-High God! Heir to the Throne of Grace! Sister to my Savior! No weapon formed against me shall prosper! Thank you Lord that you bless whatsoever I set my hands to do to prosper, in the name of Jesus!" Instantly, the feeling of being in the doldrums goes away, every time. Pray it and mean it.

## RECOGNIZE GOD'S VOICE

As the Lord leads and guides you, you may hear Him give you small steps, such as, "Go here; go there. Call this person; call that person. Say this; say that." He may give you an image of something that you don't understand yet. You may not recognize it is the Lord speaking to you; you may think it is simply your mind thinking these things. Your first reaction may be, "I don't have to go there." "I don't have to call them." "I don't have to go to that meeting." "I don't have to apologize to them." "I don't have to pay that back."

Be careful! That "I don't have to" voice is NOT the voice of the Lord. That type of response stems from rebellion and is of the devil; it is not of God. How can you tell? God does not talk like that! The Lord's voice is always soft, gentle, leading, and encouraging. The adversary is loud, bold, enticing, and discouraging. Moreover, the devil attacks you in your mind. He tries to influence your thoughts. He wants you to think it was You who said, "I don't have to go there." The devil doesn't want you to realize the 'thought' is him trying to influence you. If he can control your thoughts, he can control you.

> *The Lord's voice is always soft, gentle, leading and encouraging. The adversary is loud, bold, enticing, and discouraging.*

The "I don't have to..." used to happen with me. The Lord told me to call a person. I thought it was just me thinking to call them. I did not want to call them, so I thought to myself, "I don't have to call that person." One day, after it had happened again, I abruptly realized, "Janice, shut up! That's not God, because God doesn't talk like that!" This was an illumination to me that caused me to realize I HAD to change. The next time I heard that still small voice, say, "Call that person," I MADE MYSELF call them! I made myself obey the voice of the Lord. The beautiful thing is, when I made the call, the whole conversation turned out to be a blessing to ME! That call was entirely meant to bless ME! I was amazed. I thought, Oh! Okay, so THIS is how it works! The illumination that the soft voice was God's voice, and the blessing I received from that phone call, made it easier to obey the next time I heard that still small voice. Obedience became an automatic response. Every time I obeyed, and every time I was blessed.

When we first start walking with the Lord, and He tells us to do something, our flesh — our carnal nature — will NOT want to do it. You must MAKE your mind and body obey and do what the Lord says.

Obedience brings the reward. I was rewarded tremendously for making that phone call, even though my mind was saying, "I don't have to ..."

You must stop every negative thought before it takes hold. II Cor. 10:5 tells us to cast down "imaginations and every high thing that exalts itself against the knowledge of God, and bring into captivity every thought to the obedience of Christ." Stop ungodly thoughts. Do not let them linger.

God speaks to you in your heart. The condition of your heart is key. "Blessed are the pure in heart: for they shall see God" (Matt. 5:8). God cannot use a bitter heart. The Lord loves a pure heart. That is why the Word says, "Keep thy heart with all diligence; for out of it are the issues of life" (Prov. 4:23). Only a pure heart receives its desires.

Thoughts like "I don't have to apologize" stem from the adversary, presenting options opposite to what the Lord would have you do. You may not even recognize it is the adversary attempting to dissuade you from doing what that still small voice instructed you to do. You may think it was just you, having your own thoughts. That is why the devil attacks in the mind, hoping you think it is just your thought and not him persuading.

*The devil attacks you in your mind. God speaks to you in your heart.*

Remember, the adversary's primary goal is to keep you from obeying the Lord. He does not care what it will take to pull you off course. He will present one thing after the other to persuade you to do anything that does not please God. He will present and try to persuade repeatedly, as long as you listen and respond. He wants to distract you from doing what the Lord would have you do. You must learn to disdain the distractions; see the distractions for the evil intent that they are. **Distractions are a tool of the adversary; resist them at all costs.** Remember, "Submit yourselves therefore to God. Resist the devil and he will flee" (Jas. 4:7).

The key is OBEY TODAY! Every day, bring your flesh under subjection and **make it obey** the Will of God!

# Chapter 3

# ALLOW GOD TO MATURE YOU

Before we mature in Jesus Christ, we are not fit to do the work of the Lord. Our rebellious nature rebels against the Lord. The Lord is the Master Potter, always shaping and molding us to become whom He created us to be. We were "born in sin and shaped in iniquity" (Ps. 51:5). We all were born with the sin of Adam flowing in our blood. That means the condition in which we were born is a long way from being whom God desires us to be. Now, the Lord wants to mature us beyond our natural rebellious condition. The Lord wants us to "grow up into Him" (Eph. 4:15). The Lord wants us to take on the ways of Christ. The Lord wants to do a work in us so that He can then do a work through us.

## PURGE, PRUNE AND PERFECT

God will purge, prune, and perfect us IF and only IF we invite Him to do so and IF we allow Him to do the work in us to make us spiritually mature. Allow the Lord to purge, prune, and perfect you. Submission is an act of your will. The Lord wants to purge, prune, and perfect you, but you must want Him to do the work in you to perfect you. When Scripture says we were born in sin and shaped in iniquity, it means we were born with the sin-filled DNA of Adam running through our veins. Every human has the sin-filled blood of Adam. The Word tells us, "In your flesh dwelleth no good thing" (Rom. 7:1d). Our "flesh" is our carnal nature, the sensual part of who we are. But the real YOU is a spirit, created in the image of God. "God created man in His own image" (Gen. 1:27). "God is a Spirit, and those who worship Him, must worship in spirit and in truth" (John 4:24).

## PURGE:

We cannot worship God with a sensual nature. We must allow God to purge it from us. When you are sick with toxins in your body, they must be purged before you can fully heal. Before we accept Christ, we all have worldly toxins in our body that cause us to succumb to the adversary and to follow worldly ways. When we allow the Lord to purge the worldly toxins, He will remove and eradicate those thoughts, desires, and sensual ways that draw us away from Him. This will not be an overnight process. There will even be battles between your flesh and your spirit. Your flesh may really want to hang on to some of those thoughts and desires. You will have to choose Jesus over your desires. Simply make up your mind to submit to the Lord and not to sin.

## RENEW YOUR MIND

If you do not control your thoughts, your mind will take you places you never intended to go. Even while praying, your mind will wander off to thoughts that have absolutely nothing to do with your prayer. During prayer, you may find yourself thinking about things for which you have to ask the Lord to forgive you. You must control your mind! Control your mind by controlling your thoughts. As an ungodly thought begins to emerge, stop it in its tracks! Tell your mind, "We're not going there today!" Make your mind behave.

Bring your thoughts in line with the Word of God, not in line with the world. "Set your affection on things above, not on things on the earth" (Col. 3:2).

The Word tells us, "Do not be conformed to this world, but be transformed by the renewing of your mind, that ye may prove what is that good, and acceptable, and perfect, Will of God" (Rom. 12:2). If we are honest with ourselves, we know that we all can have some pretty ugly thoughts: prideful, hateful, lustful, sinful thoughts. These are carnal thoughts that do not please God. The Word says. "Where there is envying and strife, and divisions, are ye not carnal?" (1 Cor. 3:3). "The carnal mind is enmity against God." (Rom. 8:7). "To be carnally minded is death; but to be spiritually minded is life and peace." (Rom. 8:6).

To renew your mind, the Word says the kinds of things we should think about should be "true, honest, just, pure, lovely, of good report; if there be any virtue, and if there be any praise, think on these things" (Phil. 4:8). Thinking on things that are true, honest, just, pure, lovely, and of a good report focuses our thoughts on godly things, and it makes us grateful, appreciative, and thankful. It does not allow room for thoughts that are hateful, sinful, lustful, or envious.

Be anxious for nothing. Do not worry, stress, and pine over anything. Pray and seek the Lord about everything. Your stress will diminish and be replaced with peace. "Be careful for nothing; but in everything by prayer and supplication with thanksgiving let your requests be made known unto God. And the peace of God, which passeth all understanding, shall keep your hearts and minds through Christ Jesus" (Phil. 4:7–8).

Ask the Lord to renew your mind. Ask Him to search your mind and to remove any thought that does not please Him. Ask the Lord to give you "the mind of Christ" (1 Cor. 2:16). We must challenge every ungodly thought that comes to our mind. We live in an ungodly world, surrounded by ungodly TV, movies, and people. We even live in ungodly flesh. However, that is no excuse for us to be ungodly. Ungodly thoughts are going to pop into your head; they are going to come. Even amid trying to pray, an ungodly thought may pop into your head. That can happen when surrounded by a world of ungodliness. It is, therefore, essential to ask the Lord to search your mind and to remove any ungodly thought. He will bring current and past ungodly thoughts to your remembrance that do not please Him. Repent and ask the Lord to remove them. Ask Him to search your heart and to remove any ill will you harbor toward someone or any ungodly intent.

Even as the Lord removes ungodly thoughts and intent, you will also have to do some work on your own. Every time an ungodly thought pops into your head, make your thoughts obey the Word of God. "... bringing into captivity every thought to the obedience of Christ" (2 Cor. 10:5). Speak to your mind. Tell yourself, "Not today. That is not how I think anymore."

## STUBBORNNESS AND REBELLION

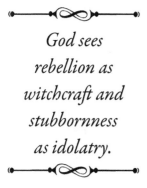

*God sees rebellion as witchcraft and stubbornness as idolatry.*

Stubbornness and rebellion ("kissing cousins") are a serious rejection of something we heard the voice of the Lord guide us to do. Stubbornness is willfully being obstinate to what the Lord said to us. It is when we know what we are to do but we object, in whole or in part, and refuse to act on it or to go forward. Rebellion is the intentional decision to defy what the Lord told us to do, often doing the opposite. Rebellion is willfully resisting the Lord and revolting against what we know we are to do. Both stubbornness and rebellion come out of the prideful nature of our flesh; they occur when we think we know what is best for us; contrary to what God said. The Word tells us, "God sees rebellion as the sin of

44

witchcraft and stubbornness as idolatry" (1 Sam. 15:23). When we rebel, God sees us as practicing witchcraft, which is a sin.

Stubbornness and rebellion are sinful. Sin brings unwanted consequences. "The wages of sin is death" (Rom. 6:23). We may not physically die when we sin, but something is going to die. We will experience the death of our potential, the death of a relationship, the death of an opportunity — something is going to die when we sin. Again, both stubbornness and rebellion come out of our own fleshly pride when we think we know more than God. We think we know what is best for ourselves more than the Creator who made us. When we are stubborn towards something the Lord tells us to do, in His sight, we are practicing idolatry. When we are rebellious towards the voice of the Lord, in His sight, we are practicing witchcraft.

Rebellion and stubbornness have no place in the life of a Christian. We cannot be stubborn or rebellious and please the Lord. When we say we love the Lord, there should be evidence of our love. When we say we know the Lord and have a relationship with the Lord, there should be evidence of our relationship. The primary evidence as to whether we know the Lord, or not, is measured in how we keep His Word. Obeying God's Will and God's Word is paramount to our Christian growth. Rebellion and stubbornness prove we do not know Him. "By this, we know that we know Him, if we keep His commandments. He who says, 'I know Him,' and does not keep His commandments, is a liar, and the truth is not in him. But, whoever keeps His Word, truly the love of God is perfected in him" (1 John 2:3–5).

## FREE WILL

God gives us free will to choose whether we will obey Him or not obey. He gives us free will to choose what we do or say, where we will go, and with whom we will go. Though He gives us free will to make our own choices, HIS WILL is that we follow His Word and obey

His Will. He says, "I have set before you life and death, blessings and cursing: therefore choose life" (Deut. 30:19). The Lord is telling us to choose life! Jesus is the Way, the Truth, and the LIFE! God is telling us to choose life through Jesus.

Regardless of what we want for ourselves, what we want is so minuscule, it is incomparable to what God wants for our lives. Our omniscient Father created us for His purpose. To discover that purpose, and to walk in that purpose, we must decrease our will and allow God's Will to increase in us.

### Prayer of Submission

Dear Heavenly Father, in the name of Jesus, I submit myself as an empty and open vessel for you to use as you choose. I decrease so that you increase in me, through the indwelling power of your blessed Holy Spirit.

I have no will but to do Your Will.

I have no desire but to please you.

Thy Will be done, and thy Will alone be done in me, with me, by me, for me, to me and through me, to your glory and to your honor.

In Jesus' name, I pray. Amen.

Just as Jesus sacrificed His life for us, we must sacrifice our life for Him. You must die to self. Put your personal agenda down and submit to the plan God has for you. By an act of your own will, you must "choose life" and choose to submit to and follow the path and plan God has ordained for you. Day by day, task by task, ask the Lord to lead you in everything you do. Then follow as He leads.

## POSSESS YOUR REINS, CONTROL YOUR FLESH

When we were born into this flesh, "we were born in sin and shaped in iniquity" (Ps. 51:5). The sin nature of Adam has passed through generations and is in every baby birthed into this world. We have the sin nature of Adam in our blood, and that naturally causes us to want to please our flesh and not obey God. "In your flesh dwelleth no good thing" (Rom. 7:18). You cannot trust your flesh/your natural desires to make godly decisions; it cannot. God gives us free will, but your will is so strong, there is no room for God to do His Will in you. For God to use us, we must decrease so there is room for His Will to increase in us through the indwelling Power of His blessed Holy Spirit. The Holy Spirit in you, will empower you to obey the Lord and not your flesh.

Make your flesh obey. Do not obey your flesh. Your flesh has a mind of its own. Your flesh is your physical body, your natural man. YOU are spirit. You live in your body, but you are not your body. Because we live in the natural realm, our spirit needs a body to dwell here. Our body is simply the house in which our spirit dwells in this natural realm. It is a vessel for our spirit to move about in this natural world. Our body is our transportation, like a car or horse. You must learn to possess your reins; take control of your body, or it will take control of you.

Think of your body as your horse, your mode of transportation. Imagine a cowboy on a horse traveling from Baltimore to New York. The cowboy does not take the reins of the horse; he simply sits on the horse's back and allows the horse to trot along. The horse, not having any direction from the cowboy, meanders wherever it wants to go. The cowboy is more likely to end up in Atlanta rather than his destination of New York. Likewise, your body — as your horse — has a mind of its own and will take you wherever IT wants to go. You must possess your reins. Just as the cowboy must take the reins of his horse to guide it in the direction he wants to travel, so must you possess the reins of your flesh and make it go in the right direction, go to the right places, do the right things, eat the right things, say the right things, and be with the right people.

There is a constant battle between our flesh and our spirit. "For the flesh lusteth against the Spirit, and the Spirit against the flesh: and these are contrary to the other" (Gal. 5:17). Our spirit continuously wants to do the things that please the Lord. Our flesh, on the other hand, is at enmity with the Lord. It wants nothing to do with the Lord. "In your flesh dwelleth no good thing" (Rom. 7:18). There is nothing about this vessel, this flesh we live in, that wants to please God. Your flesh wants lustful things like "fornication, adultery, idolatry, hatred, strife, envy, wrath, and such like these" (Galatians 5:19). Remember, you are spirit! God is Spirit and He made us in His image. "God is spirit: and they that worship Him, must worship Him in spirit and in truth (John 4:24). Our spirit dwells in our body. We are not our body; our body is our home on earth, the place our spirit dwells. We must take dominion over our flesh (our body) and make it obey what the Word tells us to do. "Our spirit is willing, but our flesh is weak" (Matt. 26:41). So, we must strengthen our spirit daily: read the Word daily, pray in the Spirit daily, and pray daily to ensure we feed, nourish, and strengthen our spirit. Our flesh makes sure we feed it every day. It even reminds us that it is hungry when our stomach growls. Our body demands food every day; sometimes it demands specific foods, and we often succumb to the demands of our flesh. That is a recipe for disaster. Never let your flesh run the show. Your flesh is not the decision-maker; you are! You must always maintain control of your flesh and possess your reins. "Walk in the Spirit, and you shall not fulfil the lust of the flesh" (Gal. 5:16).

## BRING YOUR FLESH UNDER SUBJECTION

Bringing your flesh under subjection means denying your natural cravings, habits, hobbies, and addictions that do not line up with the

Word and Will of God. You may literally need to tell your flesh, "No! You are not having that anymore. You are not going there anymore. You are not going to hang with them anymore." Your flesh will kick and buck, just like an untamed horse, but be persistent. YOU (your spirit) have dominion over your flesh, but you must take dominion. You must feed your spirit every day, just as you feed your body. Nourish your spirit with the Word of God daily. Pray daily and pray in the Spirit daily.

Imagine two lions, each caged. The lions are of the same age and physical stature. One lion receives 30 pounds of steak to eat every day; the other gets a bowl of goulash. The steak-eating lion is allowed out of the cage daily for exercise; the other stays in the cage, always. After one month, these lions must fight each other. Which lion do you think will win? The one who is well-fed and exercised will certainly have the advantage and ultimately win the battle. The same holds true for the battle between your flesh and your spirit. Your spirit and your body are the two lions at odds with each other. Your body wars against your spirit. If you want to win the war against your flesh, your spirit must be fed the Word of God daily. Your spirit must exercise in the Word of God by applying the Word to your daily living. Your spirit must always be stronger than your flesh.

Just as you feed your body daily, you must feed your spirit daily. Just as you exercise your body, you must exercise your spirit. Talk to God, thank Him, praise Him, and ask Him for guidance. Read the Bible. Pray. Ask Him questions on how to handle a situation. Ask Him to show you how to do a project you need to finish. He will answer you. He will also give you tasks to do that will be greater than what you may think you can handle. Do them anyway; He will lead you through the process if you ask Him. That is exercising your

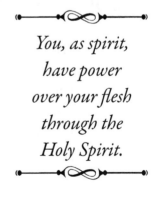

*You, as spirit, have power over your flesh through the Holy Spirit.*

spirit. Actively engage in talking with the Lord and do what He leads you to do.

YOU ARE SPIRIT! With Jesus as your Savior and Lord, and after you have received the indwelling Power of the Holy Spirit, you have the same power that raised Jesus from the dead living inside of you. You have control of your flesh and your mind. You, as spirit, have power over your flesh, through the Holy Spirit.

## PRUNE

The Lord wants to prune us; to trim and snip off those habits, hobbies, and addictions that continue to pull us toward the world's ways. As Christians, we cannot be a credible witness to the lost if we are hanging with the lost, doing the same habits and addictions as they do. By an act of your own will, you must let the habits, hobbies, and addictions go. You must also let go of friends who continue those habits. You must choose to please the Lord instead of pleasing your flesh.

*You must choose to please the Lord above pleasing your flesh.*

## COME OUT OF THE WORLD

As Christians, we are in this world but not of this world. We must come out of the world and be separate. Whatever the world is doing is a signal to the Christian of what we should not do. We cannot follow the world and follow the Word. "Do not love the world or the things in the world. If anyone loves the world, the love of the Father is not in him. For all that is in the world — the lust of the flesh, the lust of the eyes, and the pride of life — is not of the Father but is of the world.

And the world is passing away, and the lust thereof: but he who does the Will of God abides forever" (1 Jn 2:15–17).

Coming out of the world means letting go of ungodly habits, hobbies, addictions that do not glorify God. To grow spiritually you must also let go of carnal people, places, and activities that shape your current lifestyle. A few examples are listed here:

Ungodly TV shows and movies. Unsaved people may choose to watch X-rated movies and R-rated TV shows; Christians should not. Some TV shows boast of the devil; they have characters playing the role of the devil on regular episodes. Some shows appear to be cute little sitcoms, but children are witches who can make bullies disappear. Some shows glorify wealth and greed and disparage anyone who is not wealthy. There are TV shows where lust and bedroom scenes abound, killings are normal, and profanity is commonplace. Christians should watch none of these types of shows.

Your eyes are the window to your soul. Be careful what you let your eyes see, for what your eyes see feeds your soul. If you watch a thing often enough, and long enough, it will certainly become normal to you. Normal is acceptable. Acceptable things are embraced, and often replicated; like couples living together without being married, men with men or women with women. Come out of the world and be separate. The Lord made you to be distinctively different from the world. As a Christian, you are to be an example of Christ to the lost. As a Christian, you are not to follow the world; you are to be a Christ-like example to the world. When a Christian hangs out with unsaved people and does the same sinful activities that the unsaved do, he presents himself as a hypocrite to the unsaved, not an example. Your sinful actions may cause the unsaved to question the point of salvation.

Carnal music. What you let your ears hear is a barometer of your spiritual growth. Music is an influencer. Whatever music you listen to will most definitely influence your mood, your attitude, and your behavior. A Christian who listens to carnal music with profanity or sexual innuendoes is still a babe in Christ; he is born of God's Spirit, yet he needs to be matured and perfected. "Abstain from fleshly lusts, which war against the soul" (1 Peter 2:11). If you are filled with God's Spirit and led by His Spirit, it should grieve your spirit to listen to this type of music.

Years ago, I was with a friend who liked to listen to a radio station that played soulful music on the evening segment. As the radio DJ was signing off, the DJ said, in his deep, sultry voice, "Thank you for letting me play with your emotions." I was stunned! That DJ might as well have reached his hand through the radio and slapped me in my face, because that is exactly what his comment did. It was an illumination. I realized at that moment that playing with our emotions is exactly what the DJ intended to do. Playing with our emotions is exactly their mission. Why should we allow someone to manipulate us through music? Why would we allow ourselves to be subjected to emotional manipulation by someone we don't even know? Why would we listen to someone who is paid to appeal to our flesh in a way that draws us into a certain mood they want to create. This is not God, and it is not of God.

I gave up listening to the radio. I even gave up listening to Gospel radio stations because even if the songs were okay, the DJ would often say off-center comments or jokes. Or, there would be banter in the studio about a topic, and while everyone was laughing, the conversation itself was offensive. The commercials would be about liquor, a secular club, a secular special event, or something else that was not of God. It all grieved my spirit.

For 10 years, I did not listen to the radio. Then, one day while riding with my son-in-law, he had his radio tuned to a contemporary Christian music radio station. I was borrowing the car for the weekend and decided to let the radio continue to stay on and play. The music ministered to my spirit. I enjoyed the music so much that when I returned the car, I thanked my son-in-law for exposing me to such inspiring music. He did not realize he had done anything special; the station was simply what they listened to in their cars. That station (WGTS 91.9 FM) is now the only radio station I listen to. I play it in my car and in my home every day. I even have the music playing softly in the background while I watch television. The music ministers to me. The station is listener-supported so there are no commercials or advertisements. As a listener-supporter, I make a small monthly contribution to the station because daily I get so much out of their music ministry.

Carnal people. You will never rise above the company you keep. To grow spiritually, do not continue to socialize with people who are in the world, doing worldly things. You may find yourself right back in the game of doing worldly things yourself, even if it is just to maintain your friendship. You may not have to stop being friends but stop following their lead in doing things that you know do not please the Lord.

To gain spiritual maturity, surround yourself with people who are striving to please the Lord. Surround yourself with people who are more spiritually mature than you are. When you want to mature spiritually yet your friends are still in the world, constantly doing worldly things, their behaviors and choices will lure you right back into the world with them. You must let them go! Surround yourself with people whose life already exemplifies Christ. These people will be able to share insight with you on how they grew and on how God was faithful in seeing them through issues and challenges. They can be mentors and role models to you. You need godly friends and godly examples. "Iron sharpens iron; so a man sharpens the countenance of his friend" (Prov. 27:17). Learning through natural examples of God's faithfulness to others will encourage you in your walk. You can have exciting explorations in Christian fellowship. You are free to do anything you want, except sin. Christian fellowship provides opportunities that will stretch and strengthen your spiritual maturity. Your spiritual maturity may in turn strengthen someone else. Fellowship with other Christians is a spiritually and naturally enriching experience.

Places. Carnal places present a sensual environment that will draw you in before you realize it is too late. Carnal places include nightclubs, house parties, a sensual friend's house, gambling casinos, and any place where carnal music plays, drugs are plenteous, or liquor flows. Carnal places can even include a movie, either in a theater or in someone's home. If the movie is full of profanity, sex, and killing, does it please the Lord? If you are watching it, are you pleasing the Lord? These are all worldly activities and behaviors of those who are unsaved. Christians cannot do and behave as the unsaved. The Word says we are "the temple of the living God, and God will dwell in us" (2 Cor. 6:16). If God dwells in you, would you want to take God into a nightclub, a sensual friend's house, a gambling casino, or someone else's bed? The Lord tells us, "Come out from among them, and be ye separate, says the Lord and touch not the unclean thing, and I will receive you. And will be a Father to you, and ye shall be my sons and daughters, says the Lord Almighty" (2 Cor. 6:17–18). Come out of the world!

Activities. In Christian fellowship, you are free to do any sport or activity you would like, as long as you do not sin. From football to skiing, chess to charades, theatre to museums, fishing to boating, cook-outs to brunches, all options are open to you for great fun and excitement, as long as you do not sin. Set your heart to please the Lord, and it will become easy to select fun-filled events or activities to enjoy.

Halloween. One of the primary activities that a Christian should never participate in is Halloween. Halloween is a celebration of evil. It is one of the four major holidays for witchcraft. October 31st is the one day when the help of the devil is most sought. Do not let the commercialization of this satanic day fool you. It is a festive day for those who worship the devil. If you do not worship the devil, do not participate in Halloween in any manner whatsoever. Do not let your children wear costumes, even at home. Even if the costume is an angel or an astronaut, if you allow your child to wear it on Halloween, you are teaching your children to celebrate Satan. Do not purchase candy to give out to children who come to your door. Keep your porch light off so 'trick-or-treaters' skip your house.

A Christian should never celebrate Halloween, no matter who else does, whether it be your best friends, your neighbors, or other family members. Do not celebrate Halloween no matter how much fun it appears, no matter how much your children plead with you, and no matter who invites you to the party. If you do not want to be associated as a Satanist, do not celebrate Satan. Halloween is a distraction from the Will of God. Disdain the distraction. Be a credible witness to your children, your friends, and your neighbors. Stand up for Jesus who gave His life to save yours from this very evil. Be Christ-like and resist the world's temptation.

## DO NOT LET OTHERS PUSH YOUR BUTTONS

As we progress through life, we are most assuredly going to encounter people who will annoy us, irritate us, anger us, or simply pluck our nerves. It happens to everyone; that is life. As Christians, how we handle ourselves when someone angers us matters. We cannot treat them as they treat us. We cannot let them have a piece of our mind. We cannot tell them off and throw a few four-letter words in to make sure they get our point. No, we cannot do that. As Christians, we cannot respond the same way as those who do not know Christ may respond. We cannot respond the way WE used to respond before our relationship with the Lord. We must, continuously, possess our reins, control our flesh, and make it come under subjection to the Word and Will of God. We must be credible witnesses, all day, every day.

Why do you respond the way you do when someone does or says something you don't like? What is it that makes you respond in a terse or inflammatory manner? Examine yourself. How we act is important, but how we react is even more important. We plan how we are going to act, but we do not plan how we are going to react. When we lash out at others and yell because we are being yelled at, we are allowing others to "push our buttons"; we are allowing someone else's actions to throw us off-course. When others can cause us to act in ways that are contrary to how we normally conduct ourselves, we are revealing a flaw in our character and a blemish in our heart. God looks at the heart. He looks at our motivation in saying or doing everything. **Never let others push your buttons.** You must be in control of your buttons. Caution: Slacking off from your daily devotions is another way to leave yourself vulnerable to allowing someone else to get under your skin and push your buttons. Be steadfast in your daily devotion.

Imagine that your belly button is your emotional button. Guard it! It is your button. Do not let others push your button and cause you to act out of your Christian character. Rather, see the person for where they are. Recognize they are in some type of emotional pain or anger. Have compassion for the person because they are in such a dark and ugly place. You would not want to be in that position, so pray for them. Amid them being mean or ugly, pray for them. Pray fervently for them. Pray within; do not let them know you are praying. Matthew 5:44 tells us to "pray for them which despitefully use you and persecute you." Your prayer for those who are spiteful will be a tremendous blessing to You. Praying for them will guard your heart; it will help you remain in right standing with the Lord. You will be able to be a blessing to them if no more than through prayer.

I used to wonder why people would be so mean, selfish, or unkind to me. I would ask the Lord why they would act that way. One day, the Lord told me, "I hold you one hundred percent accountable for everything you say, everything you do, how you act, and how you react. But

I do not hold you at all accountable for what anyone else says or does." This was extremely liberating to me! No longer did I focus on what others did or why others acted the way they did. When the Lord illuminated this to me, it made me focus my attention on ME. It made me focus on the intent of my heart, my words, my actions, and more importantly, on my reactions. It made me guard my heart more. I was able to "see" the other person for who they were and the state they were in. I could not get upset or angry by what they said. I could see that they were acting that way because they were in such a dark and ugly place. I felt sorry for them during their fury because I would not want to be in that dark and ugly place. I felt compassion enough to pray for them, right then and there, amid their ugliness. I never prayed aloud; I prayed quietly to myself that God would heal their heart and give them peace. Praying for them kept me in peace. Praying for them kept my heart pure.

*Message from the Lord: "I hold you one hundred percent accountable for everything you say, everything you do, how you act, and how you react. But I do not hold you at all accountable for what anyone else says or does."*

Our reactions tell more about our hearts than our actions. We tend to plan our actions; we plan how we are going to say or handle a thing. However, what about when we are caught off guard? What about when someone comes out of nowhere with inflammatory comments or behavior? At this point, we are in reaction mode. It is our reaction to what others say or do that reflects our heart condition. Carnal reactions cause us to see a glaring blemish in our character. We must always remain in control of ourselves.

If you are okay with God, you are okay. Do not waste time wondering why people did or said mean things. Instead, just make sure you stay in right standing with the Lord. You will be able to see that the person who is being mean is really in a dark and ugly place. They are speaking and acting out of hurt and out of the pain they feel at that moment. They are allowing the adversary to use them to do his work, to hurt your feelings enough to provoke you to act out of your hurt and pain. Never let the actions of others throw you off-course.

## LOOK BEYOND THEIR FAULT AND SEE THEIR NEED

One of the primary lessons I learned from my mother in handling difficult people, was to look beyond their fault and to see their need. At one time or another, we all go through personal or emotional challenges that cause pain. Jesus gave us His Holy Spirit as our Comforter

*Look beyond their fault and see their need.*

for such a time as this. The comfort of the Holy Spirit is one of the blessings and benefits of salvation. Those who do not know the Lord go through personal and emotional pain, as well, yet they do not have the Comforter to shield them from the pain. Babes in Christ have yet to recognize they can call upon the Lord for comfort. People in pain act out. We must look beyond their fault and see their need. Do not focus so much on what they are doing or how they are acting. Focusing on how they are acting will cause you to miss the point. Seek to understand why they are acting that way. Perhaps God allows us to experience hurtful situations because He wants us to be able to be a blessing to the one who is really in pain. When your heart is in line with the Lord, He can use the Comforter in you to comfort others. As you are mentally praying for the situation before you, the Lord may tell you to say something, to offer something, or to do something that will be exactly what the person needs at the time.

## GROW UP INTO HIM

Scripture says that we are to "grow up into Him" (Eph. 4:15). We are each on our own personal growth journey. Where are you in your spiritual growth and maturity? We must become mature Christians so the Lord can use us. We cannot remain babes in Christ. We must become strong enough to fight the good fight of faith, strong enough for spiritual warfare, strong enough to be soldiers on the battlefield for the Lord.

Consider spiritual growth as being similar to the school system. Children as young as four years old start pre-K, then there's kindergarten, elementary school, middle school, high school, and then college undergrad, grad school, and doctorate levels of educational accomplishments. We frequently see people attain multiple degrees, perhaps a Ph.D. and then a master's degree in a different field. Each of these educational categories is made up of various grade levels, or years, such as elementary school, middle school, and so forth. Consider how many grade levels or years there are between pre-K and Ph.D.: at least 22 levels. These different levels give us an idea of how much the student has learned or has educationally matured. For example, we would certainly expect a tenth-grader to be more mature, more prepared, and more learned than a second-grader.

Our spiritual growth also has multiple levels. No one can number the levels or tell you when one level ends and the next level picks up, except of course, the Lord Himself. If we likened our spiritual growth and maturity to educational levels, where do you think you would be on the spiritual maturity growth chart?

No matter how spiritually mature you are, there is another level higher for you to reach. Never think you know it all! That is a set up for disaster. Always remain teachable. When you stop learning, you stop growing; anything not growing is dying. Continue to grow spiritually; choose wisely the material things, the people, the places, and even the thoughts you use. Be cognizant of every person, activity, habit, and possession you incorporate into your life; ensure that each one helps you to glorify the Lord. The more you grow spiritually, the more the Lord can and will use you.

## TRUST AND OBEY

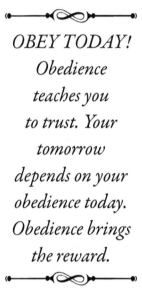

*OBEY TODAY!*
*Obedience*
*teaches you*
*to trust. Your*
*tomorrow*
*depends on your*
*obedience today.*
*Obedience brings*
*the reward.*

We always hear "trust and obey" in that order, with trust referenced before obey. However, the manifestation of trust comes in the reverse order. You must obey FIRST! Obedience teaches you to trust. Obey the Lord. Obey His Word. Obey His direction. Obey the Lord even when what He instructs you to do does not make sense to your natural mind. "The natural man receiveth not the things of the Spirit of God; for they are foolishness to him: neither can he know them, because they are spiritually discerned" (1 Cor. 2:14). Do not rely on your mind or intellect to understand why the Lord is telling you to do something. The natural mind cannot comprehend the things of God. We must obey, period!

Obey the Lord whenever He gives you instructions, whether you understand why you are to do the task or not. Your understanding is not what is important here; your obedience is. Regardless of what you think, obey. The Lord is your Father, and He loves you. He knows more than you do, and He will never lead you astray. The more you obey the Lord, the more you will see blessings coming directly from your obedience. Obedience brings the reward. "He is a rewarder of them that diligently seek Him" (Heb. 11:6b). The more you obey, the more you will see God's faithfulness towards you, and the more you will learn to trust the Lord. The more you trust the Lord, the more you will obey Him. You will begin to know you can depend on Him because you will have seen His faithfulness to you. Do not worry about the long-term or what the future holds; leave that to God. Just obey whatever the Lord tells you to do today. Do that every day. Develop the mantra "OBEY TODAY!" Obedience only works for today. Your obedience today is helping to prepare you for the work God wants you to do in your tomorrows. Your tomorrow depends on your obedience today. Your obedience today is teaching you to be steadfast; this is a character trait you will need later to handle what God knows is coming down the line.

When the Lord tells you to do something, it may make absolutely no sense to you at the time. As His child, you are to obey. The Lord wants you to obey His Commandments, His Word, and His Will. When you said you were His child, you asked Him to lead you. When you ask the Lord to lead you, surrender your will to His Will, completely. You must <u>allow</u> the Lord lead to you. The Lord is a gentleman; He will not force His Will upon you. You must make a personal decision to submit your body, your mind, and your will to your Heavenly Father and to the leading of Jesus' Blessed Holy Spirit.

When the Lord tells you something to do, most often, you will not want to do it. Your flesh, your natural man, will not want to obey whatever the Lord wants. Your "spirit indeed is willing but the flesh is weak." (Matt. 26:41). Our flesh is always at enmity with God. "In our flesh dwelleth no good thing" (Rom. 7:18). We must put our flesh under subjection to our spirit and make our flesh (ourselves) obey the Word and the Will of the Lord.

In my earlier years, when the Lord would tell me to do this, do that, go here or go there, I didn't recognize it was the Lord telling me to do these things. I just thought it was my own thoughts. So, I would say to myself, "Humph! I don't have to do this or that. I don't have to go here or there." And, I wouldn't. Then one day, I heard again, "Call this person." As my flesh (my natural man) began to rise and say, "I don't have to call this person," I stopped in my tracks! It dawned on me that stubborn voice was not God! God doesn't talk like that! I realized that was the voice of the adversary trying to dissuade me from doing what that still, quiet voice of God was telling me to do.

I certainly did not want to call that person, but when I recognized it was the voice of the Lord, I HAD to do it. I knew making the call was the instruction the Lord was telling me to do. I MADE myself do it! I made my flesh obey. I asked the Lord to guide me in what to say, and I picked up the phone and called the person. When the conversation was over, and I hung up the phone, I was so overwhelmed with delight that I flopped back in my chair, praising the Lord and telling Him how awesome He is. The conversation with the person turned out to be a tremendous blessing to ME. I thought, "So this is how it works!" I was so thrilled with the unexpected beneficial results of the conversation that I made up my mind I could no longer listen to that obnoxious voice telling me I did not have to do something. Right then, I determined in my heart, and committed to the Lord, that from that day on, I would obey His still, quiet voice.

## OBEDIENCE

Many times, we miss opportunities for God to bless us. God often gives us opportunities to demonstrate our love for Him, our obedience to Him, and our spiritual growth and maturity. Every time the Holy Spirit nudges you to help someone, call someone, give to someone, or pray for someone, it is an opportunity for YOU to get blessed. Doing when prompted is God offering you an opportunity

*Growth comes from applying God's Word, not just hearing it.*

to show your spiritual growth and maturity, an opportunity to pass another test.

Be sensitive to the leading of the Lord. The longer you delay responding to the Lord's leading, the longer you delay your own growth and your own maturity. The more you delay, the longer it will take for you to pass the test and move to the next higher level of spiritual purpose. Growth comes from applying God's Word, not just hearing it.

Obedience brings the reward. The reward is trust. Trust is born out of our obedience. The more you obey, the more faithful you will see the Lord to be. The more faithful you see the Lord to be, the more you know He will be with you when you obey. The more you know the Lord will be with you when you obey, the more you will trust Him. The more you trust Him, the bolder you will be in witnessing for Him. The more you trust Him, the stronger you will be in carrying out His instructions to you, for then you know the Lord will do the work through you.

You trust God only as much as you obey Him. You love God only as much as you obey Him. Saying you love the Lord means nothing if you do not obey Him. Not obeying what the Lord tells you to do is an indication that you do not trust Him. When you trust the Lord, you will act and do, even when it is something you (your flesh) does not want to do. You must "press toward the mark for the prize of the high calling of God in Christ Jesus" (Phil. 3:14). Know that what He has in store for you at the end of this task is a far greater blessing.

## STAY IN POSITION

Obedience also includes continuing to do what the Lord leads you to do, even when things get tough, rough, and ugly. The Lord may lead you to a particular job or a certain church. You may enjoy being there in the beginning. At the church, you may enjoy the services and be drawn to the Word through the messages. You may enjoy your fellow members and become active in a ministry. Then someone does something, or says something that offends you, directly or indirectly. You pray about it and let it go. But when it happens again, you don't pray; you just get frustrated. The Sunday messages start to become a little too strict for you. The pastor now says members should not drink alcohol, of any type, not even wine. You think that's a bit much and frown at the idea. Then you don't get acknowledged for a project you completed. Next, someone else receives a leadership position who has much less tenure and experience than you have. You take all of it personally and decide this is no longer the church for you. You decide to leave and join another church. Stop! Not so fast.

At each of these incidents, which may have looked like downward turns for you, did you pray? Did you ask the Lord to show you what to do? Did you ask the Lord to show you what He wanted you to see, to know, to understand? When the Lord sends you to a place, He has a reason for sending you there. You must learn what He wants you to learn; you must bless whom He wants you to bless; you must grow how He wants you to grow. When the Lord sends you to a place, there is work He wants you to do. Perhaps you are to be a blessing to someone you have not encountered as of yet. Perhaps someone is to be a blessing to you. You cannot quit and leave just because things are not going the way you want. Things are never going to go one hundred percent the way you want, no matter where you go. When the Lord leads you to go somewhere, a job, church, or other assignments, you must remain in position until the Lord gives you a different set of instructions. Quitting or leaving is rebelling against the Lord. It is a self-righteous move indicating you believe you know better for yourself than God does. That is a detrimental mindset. The Lord will send you to many places. Stay in position; your blessing is there.

## PERFECT

The Lord wants to perfect us. Jesus wants to do a work in us so that we become spiritually mature enough for Him to do a work through us. As the Lord perfects you, He will show you things about yourself that do not please Him. It may not be anything sinful; it may simply be the perspective you have toward a situation, the thoughts you have about a person or group of people, the approach you take when handling a matter, your zealousness or apathy on issues. What the Lord shows you will be specifically your weaknesses and your areas of improvement. Whatever He shows you, He is showing you His desire for you to change. The Lord will not change you. Change must be an act of your will. You must seek Him and ask Him to show you how to change. He will guide you through every step and show you what to do, how to do it, when to do it, and more. You may experience hurtful realizations about yourself and have heartfelt repentance. This is good; it is a point of spiritual growth. The more hurtful realizations and heartfelt repentances, the better. Each represents spiritual growth. Following each occasion, there will be blossoming of better character, stronger faith, and a stronger desire to please the Lord.

## GUARD YOUR HEART

Guarding your heart is one of the most significant steps you can take toward spiritual maturity. God looks at the heart. Man judges another man by the outer appearance: intellect, possessions, stature, and personality. God does not see man as man does, from the outer appearance.

God looks at the heart. "For the Lord seeth not as man seeth; for man looketh on the outward appearance, but the Lord looketh on the heart" (1 Sam. 16:7). Man looks at the outer things. It does not matter to God how much money you make, your education, your career position, how fancy your car is, how big your house may be, or how much wealth you have amassed. You may have the biggest and the best of all these things, and it will mean nothing to God if you have a bitter heart, an unforgiving heart, a selfish heart, an envying heart. It will mean nothing to God if you look down on people who have less than you, who don't look like you, who are not as educated as you, who are not as good looking as you.

To keep your heart pure, ask the Lord to search your heart and remove anything that does not please Him. Ask Him to take away selfishness, boastful pride, envying, bitterness, high-mindedness, and the like. "Guard your heart with all diligence, for out of it come the issues of life" (Prov. 4:23).

> *Your barometer to determine how mature of a Christian you are is what comes out of your mouth.*

When we mistreat others, lash out in anger, feel hatred for any reason, bully or disparage others, be careful because "out of the abundance of the heart the mouth speaketh" (Matt. 12:34 and Luke 6:45) The time will come for all of us when we will be mistreated, hurt, or angered; that is life. It will happen to us all. The key is that through it all, we MUST remain who we are: Christians. If out of the abundance of the heart, the mouth speaketh, we must guard our heart, so we speak no evil and no guile to anyone. "The mouth of the righteous speaketh wisdom" (Ps. 37:30) but "the mouth of the wicked speaketh frowardness" (Prov. 10:32).

What is coming out of your mouth? Are you speaking wisdom to everyone, or are you lashing out and getting back? "For as he thinketh in his heart, so is he" (Prov. 23:7). Your heart is what God looks at. The barometer to determine how mature of a Christian you are is what comes out of your mouth. If evil is in your heart, it eventually will come out of your mouth. Bitterness and hate are not of God. Gossiping and boastful pride are not of God. If love and forgiveness are in your heart, you will be able to speak wisdom to the person who mistreated you. You will see past the mistreatment and see them for where they really are. When someone acts ugly, look beyond their fault and see their need. Many people act out of their own inner hurts and insecurities. Often, when someone lashes out at you, you are not the real target of their anger. They are simply so full of hurt or anger that it spills over to whomever may be near.

In my twenties, I was talking with my father, who was the most righteous man I have ever known. I asked him about the Lord and how to have a pure heart. I admired Daddy's wisdom and meekness. I asked him what you must do to have a pure heart. He said to **ask the Lord to search your heart and to remove anything that does not please Him**. I began to pray that prayer regularly.

**Submit Your Heart to God**

**Dear Heavenly Father, in the Name of Jesus, I submit myself to You.**

**Search my heart Lord; remove anything that does not please You. Give me a pure heart.**

**Search my mind; remove any thought that does not please You.**

**Give me the mind of Christ.**

**I have no will but to do Your Will. I have no desire but to please You.**

**Order my steps, please, Lord. Guide me in the way You would have me to go.**

**In Jesus' name, I pray. Amen.**

The Lord started to show me things in my heart that were not of Him. He showed me times when I had been bitter towards someone or when I was unforgiving. The Lord showed me things that were of me, and not of Him. By an act of my own will, I asked the Lord to remove those and anything else that did not please Him. Now, regularly, I ask the Lord to search my heart and my mind.

God only looks at the heart. Guard your heart, for out of it come the issues of life. Whatever is in your heart will eventually come out through your words and deeds. Ask the Lord to give you a pure heart. If there is any ungodly intent, anger, or bitterness in your heart toward someone, for YOUR sake, let it go. Let it go, ask God for forgiveness, and forgive the person. We cannot glorify the Lord with a bitter heart. God cannot use a bitter heart. On a regular basis, ask God to search and purify your heart. A heart filled with anger, hate, and bitterness is useless to God. A pure heart is essential to pleasing the Lord. Monitor your heart regularly. Guard your heart with all diligence.

## FASTING

Fasting is denying your flesh what it wants while providing your spirit what it needs. That is why we call it a "spiritual fast." Fasting is essential to spiritual growth and maturity and must be done with spiritual intent (not to lose weight). Fasting heightens your spiritual sensitivity. Perhaps you want to hear from the Lord on a certain matter. Perhaps you want to develop a closer relationship with the Lord. Whatever your spiritual intent may be, lift it up before the Lord while fasting. Fasting will enable you to be more discerning, perceptive and assured of your next step.

You must intentionally deny your flesh to strengthen your spirit. Your flesh is "of this world"; there is nothing spiritual about your flesh. The Word says, "In your flesh dwelleth no good thing" (Rom. 7:18). Though we all live in a body, we are spirit. Our spirit needs a body to dwell in while in this earthen realm. The person you see in the mirror is not you; it is the body where your spirit dwells. We must always remember that we are spirit. For should we forget, our flesh will indeed have its way. Your flesh has a mind of its own, and it knows what it wants. Your flesh wants whatever is contrary to the Word of God. Unless you make your flesh behave, it will have a tantrum until you give it what it wants, such as excessive food, fornication, drugs, liquor, and gambling. Denying your flesh will bring your flesh under subjection to your will. You must bring your flesh under subjection and make it obey the Word of God and submit to your spirit.

Fasting is denying your flesh. This means not having, or not doing, things that your flesh enjoys the most and that you do on a daily or regular basis. If watching TV is your thing, fast from TV for 21 days, and use that TV time to pray and exercise while you pray. If you are a big meat eater, fast from all forms of meat and seafood for 21 days, while you increase your vegetable intake. If sweets are your treat, fast from all forms of anything sweet, including sugar in your coffee, for 21 days, while switching to fruits as your dessert.

Scripture tells us of the "Daniel fast," where Daniel gave up sweets, meat, and wine for 21 days (Daniel 10:3). During the 21 days, focus your attention on reading the Bible, prayer, and meditation in the Word; "meditate therein day and night" (Josh. 1:8). Limit television and radio time to spiritual or Gospel-based programs. Search online for "the Daniel fast" for types of foods to eat and omit during your 21-day fast.

Yes, fasting may feel like sacrifice in the beginning, until you remember the sacrifice Jesus made on the cross for you. If Jesus could sacrifice His Life, surely, we can sacrifice food, TV, and activities for a season. Remembering Jesus' sacrifice on the cross will encourage you and strengthen you throughout your fast.

Fasting de-clutters the mind; it quiets the noise in your subconscious mind. As we go about our daily activities in this world, we are constantly bombarded with things of the world: ungodly people, TV, things we see or hear. Everything we see and hear can affect us in a worldly way. Like dust collects on the coffee table, things of the world can collect in our hearts even when we don't realize it. The dust will continue to build up until we remove it. As long as we are in this world, we will never totally get away from worldly things. From time to time, we must fast to rid ourselves of the "dust" that has collected on us in our normal course of living.

Carry out the Daniel fast at least once a year. Many people choose the season of Lent before Resurrection Sunday to do the Daniel fast. It is both refreshing and strengthening. Fast anytime and every time you feel something is plaguing you and you are not able to discern the cause. Fast when persecution is upon you. Fast when you need guidance and direction. In 2010, I did the Daniel fast four times within one year. That means for one-third of the year, I was fasting. Every time something troubled me, I would fast. (I share why in Chapter 4.) That one year, I grew significantly stronger spiritually.

Be sincere, committed, and deliberate in fasting. Fasting is between you and God. No one will know if you cheat except you and God. Lift up your spiritual intent before the Lord. Ask the Holy Spirit to strengthen you through the fast. Ask the Lord to show you what you need to know or to do. Fasting is an excellent tool to add to your arsenal as a soldier in the army of the Lord. Fasting will help strengthen you to fight the good fight of faith.

## RIGHTEOUSNESS

The Bible mentions righteousness 291 times: in the Old Testament, 200 times, and in the New Testament, 91 times. When the Word mentions a character trait 291 times, it must be important to God.

How important is righteousness to God? This passage makes it clear: "In this the children of God are manifest, and the children of the devil: **whosoever doeth not righteousness is not of God**, neither he that loveth not his brother" (I Jn. 3:10). Another passage makes it clear: "Little children, let no man deceive you: he that doeth righteousness is righteous, even as he is righteous" 1 Jn. 3:7). "All unrighteousness is sin" (1 Jn. 5:17).

Jesus made us the righteousness of God, so we are in right standing with God. "For he had made him to be sin for us, who knew no sin; that we might be made the righteousness of God in Him" (2 Cor. 5:21). Jesus made us right, so now we must BE right, DO right and STAY right with the Lord.

Most people stand on one verse regarding righteousness — the verse where Jesus did all the work in making us the righteousness of God. Yes, Jesus made us right with God, but we cannot rest on what Jesus did. We have a role to play as well. Jesus gave us the gift of righteousness. He put us in position to be in right standing with God. Now, it is up to us to stay right with God. We cannot do things that those in the world would do (cuss, gossip, envy, lie, cheat, gamble, fornicate, have personal agendas, etc.) and think we are OK with God. Though people all around us may do these things regularly, as mature Christians, we cannot. We are in this world, but not of this world. We cannot do as the world does. We are to set the example of a Christian and be Christ-like in our character and in our conduct, in all that we say and all that we do, how we act, and more importantly, how we react.

Righteousness is a spiritual state where the blend of multiple natural attributes combine and are reflected in our very being; it is who we have become. The combined attributes of righteousness include being virtuous, just, moral, honest, decent, and blameless. Righteousness is visible and observed through our word, conduct, attitude, action, and thought.

When we manifest the fruit of the Spirit, we will also manifest righteousness. "For the fruit of the Spirit is in all goodness, and righteousness and truth" (Eph. 5:9). "Wherefore by their fruits ye shall know them" (Matt. 7:20).

It is only through righteousness that we can please God, or serve God, or be a credible witness for God. Can we please God with bitter hearts? Can we please God with lust in our hearts? Can we please God by putting our will above His Will? Can we serve God with hate in our hearts? No; none of these is an example of the pattern that Jesus left for us to follow. None of these allows us to be a credible witness.

The Word lays out the benefits of being righteous. It is only through righteousness that we can receive the things we need. The Word says, "Seek ye first the Kingdom of God and His righteousness and all these things will be added unto you" (Matt. 6:33). This is one of those promises with a condition. We must seek FIRST the Kingdom of God and His righteousness. If we are not seeking His Kingdom and His righteousness, we are missing the mark for receiving the things we need. Sure, we can go out and buy the material things we need, but only God can provide the spiritual things we need to do His work in the Kingdom. Only the Lord can give us guidance, direction, protection, wisdom, answers, favor, and grace.

It is only through righteousness that the Lord will guide us, for the Word says, "The steps of a righteous man are ordered by the Lord" (Ps. 37:23). God is telling us that He guides His children who are right with Him, those who are in His Will. Have you ever prayed and prayed for God to help you or show you something and you never got an answer? During that time, were you right with God and in His Will? We may ask for guidance and direction, but unless we are right with the Lord (in right-standing with God), we may not receive the answer. The steps of a <u>righteous</u> man are ordered by the Lord.

Yes, Jesus made us the righteousness of God. Now, every day, we must show gratitude for His gift of righteousness and BE right, DO right, and STAY right with the Lord.

There are always options open to us and doors that will open if we stay in the path of righteousness.

## Gifts of the Spirit: Walk in your Spiritual Gifts

Our Heavenly Father has plans and a purpose for each of His children. Before we can carry out the Lord's plans for us, we must first "grow up into Him" (Eph. 4:15). He wants to teach us what we need to know to become whom He created us to be. He wants to strengthen us for the journey He has set before us.

The Lord has given each of us an assignment — a specific task He wants us to carry out. The Lord has also given each of us spiritual gifts. Our gifts are essential to us carrying out the assignment God has for us.

Your job, work experience, and college degree are not your spiritual gifts. Your talents, skills, and abilities are not your spiritual gifts. Your spiritual gifts may have nothing to do with what you chose for education or profession. Your spiritual gifts are from God, used by God, according to His purpose and for the benefit of others. We are here to be a blessing to others. Your greatest blessing to another, and the most fulfilling work you will do, will manifest when you operate in your spiritual gifts in carrying out the Lord's assignment.

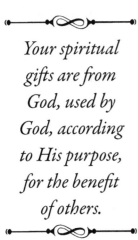

*Your spiritual gifts are from God, used by God, according to His purpose, for the benefit of others.*

There are three categories of spiritual gifts. All three categories of spiritual gifts are in the Bible. All spiritual gifts are from our Heavenly Father; they work only by the indwelling power of the Holy Spirit, and they operate at the leading of the Holy Spirit.

At my church, From the Heart Church Ministries, we are taught that the three categories of spiritual gifts are functional gifts, protectional gifts, and perfecting gifts. The church has a Perfecting Class that teaches members how to identify their functional gifts. I cannot, and would not, try to convey all that is taught in the class, but I will share some of what I have learned while operating in my gifts. Consider my overview as a glimpse into the spiritual gifts. In no way does this review address the full scope of the gifts, nor how the gifts operate.

## FUNCTIONAL GIFTS

Functional gifts enable you to function in the assignment your Heavenly Father created you to carry out. You cannot carry out your assignment without your functional gifts. All spiritual gifts work through the indwelling power of the Holy Spirit. The use of every gift manifests as a strength or a weakness in your spiritual growth. The strength of the gift is evident when you allow the Holy Spirit to operate the gift through you. The weakness is evident when you try to use the gift on your own strength. The weakness is also evident when you allow the gift to work you, rather than you working the gift.

Everyone has at least one functional gift. Many people have more than one gift. Some people have all seven functional gifts.

Functional gifts are in Romans 12:6–8 and include:

1.  The Gift of Prophesy
2.  The Gift of Ministering (Service)
3.  The Gift of Teaching
4.  The Gift of Exhortation
5.  The Gift of Giving
6.  The Gift of Leadership
7.  The Gift of Mercy

I have three functional gifts, to my knowledge: exhortation, leadership and mercy. I say "to my knowledge" because the realization that I had each of these three gifts came at different stages of my spiritual growth and walk with the Lord. In fact, I have taken the Perfecting Class three times, and with each new class, I recognized that I had an additional gift. Each of these gifts come instinctively to me. I do not think about the gift, when to use it, or how to use it. I simply ask the Lord, daily, to fill me afresh with His Holy Spirit. I submit myself and my gifts (the Lord's gifts to me) to the Holy Spirit daily and ask that God's Will be done.

Exhortation. The exhorter loves to encourage others. The exhorter can see the potential in others and thrives on working with someone to draw out their potential and to have others realize their potential. The exhorter speaks from the heart. They may not plan what they are going to say; they open their mouths and expect the Holy Spirit to speak. The exhorter is fulfilled when they see others thrive after using the guidance and encouragement they received. The weakness of the exhorter (when working on our own) is that we try to help when help is not wanted. The exhorter may also try to hold on to a negative relationship, hoping to help the person for the better. We cannot want something for others more than they want it for themselves.

Leadership. God shows the leader the big picture. The leader relies on the Lord for direction, wisdom, guidance, and provision. The leader functions as a servant leader and serves those the Lord sends to help. The leader walks in what the Lord leads them to do and does so with humility coupled with a holy boldness. The leader is Christ-confident in what the Lord wants done and has a blessed assurance that the Lord will do the work through him. The leader's commitment to the Lord's instructions draws others to follow. The leader submits himself to the

Lord because he knows the work will be done, only as the Lord leads, directs and empowers.

Mercy. Mercy is compassion in action. The person with the gift of mercy will do all they can to help another. They will sacrifice for themselves if it means being able to bless someone else. Mercy will think of the needs of others first. When the person with mercy uses mercy outside of the leading of the Holy Spirit, others will consider their kindness as weakness and will take full advantage.

Remember, everyone has at least one functional gift. You MUST learn what your functional gifts are and how to work your gifts. If you do not work your gift, the gift will work you. The gifts work even if you don't realize you have them. The problem is, the gift will work You, until you learn how to work the gift. When the gift works you, there is never a productive outcome. I learned this the hard way. I was being kind and godly, and thought I was doing something good. The challenge was, Mercy was working me to the max. I did not realize I had the gift of mercy. Mercy worked me because I didn't realize I had the gift, so I didn't know how it worked. I failed the test three times in a row before learning what I needed to learn for me to work the gift of Mercy instead of the other way around. I share details of how I failed the three tests in Chapter Five.

Learn what your Functional gifts are. You will need them to function in the assignments and tasks God has ordained for you.

## PROTECTIONAL GIFTS

God uses protectional gifts to protect His people — protection from others, from a situation, from an endeavor, or from things to come.

Protectional gifts, found in 1 Corinthians 12:8–10, include:

1. Word of Wisdom
2. Word of Knowledge
3. Gift of Faith
4. Gift of Healing
5. Working of Miracles
6. Gift of Prophecy
7. Discerning of Spirits
8. Tongues
9. Interpretation of Tongues

I have three protectional gifts: the gift of faith, the gift of prophecy and discerning of spirits.

<u>Gift of Faith</u>. I did not recognize that I had this gift until I had gone through many trials and tribulations with my head lifted up and my hand in God's hand. I was consistently obedient. The Lord was consistently faithful. This birthed my trust and faith. The gift of faith strengthens you to take on a task, knowing you know nothing about how to carry it out, but you know the Lord will lead. The Lord has led me to take on many major programs in areas where I had no prior experience. However, I knew that if God said to do it, He would lead me through it. The gift of faith enables a greater degree of obedience based on trust in the Lord. The gift of faith is operational in me daily.

*If God says do it, He will lead you through it!*

<u>Gift of Prophecy</u>. The protectional gift of prophecy is different from prophecy as a functional gift, and it is different from prophecy as a perfecting gift. As a protectional gift, prophecy warns. You will feel compelled to warn someone of a situation. You will know the need to warn is from God because the warning will be much bolder than what you

would ever say to the person. The Lord may lead you to warn someone to remove himself from a situation, a job, or an environment that is not good nor godly. In one instance, the Lord led me to warn a woman that she was to leave her job, her church, and her husband. I perceived that she was in a risky situation in each of these scenarios. I was uncomfortable telling her this but was compelled to do so. She and her husband had not lived together for years, though they "appeared" to be together on special occasions (only at church) to support their ministerial façade. I spoke this to her once, with a holy boldness that was not typically in our conversations. She knew my manner of speaking to her was different and took the warning seriously. Within a few short years, she had removed herself from her job, her husband, and relocated to another church. The gift of prophecy operates in me only occasionally.

Discerning of Spirits. The person with the gift of discerning of spirits can see past the words someone may be speaking. They can see good intentions or ill intentions from the person with whom they are interacting. Discerning of spirits can also operate in broader settings or with people whom you may hear indirectly. Discernment is a very powerful gift for me. It allows me to "see" beyond the visible and to discern what the challenge is or what the solution is for a given situation. This gift operates in me frequently.

## PERFECTING GIFTS

God uses these gifts "for the perfecting of the saints, for the work of the ministry, for the edifying of the body of Christ" (Eph. 4:12). Perfecting gifts are given to those who have a call on their lives to minister the Word of God in an official capacity, such as a pastor, minister, etc. The gifts are used to strengthen and perfect the people of God to come into the unity of the faith, to become a member of the Body of Christ, and to grow in the knowledge of the Lord.

Perfecting gifts, found in Ephesians 4:11–13, include:

1. Apostle
2. Prophets
3. Evangelists
4. Pastors and Teachers

Certainly, I do not have a calling to lead a congregation; however, I do often think I have the gift of an evangelist. I do not occupy the office of an evangelist, but I believe I have the gift. The evangelist does not have a church or congregation, but they speak the Word of God to whomever the Lord puts before them. Their congregation is whomever they encounter each day. The evangelist leads others to Christ. The evangelist can use the Word to correct those who hold beliefs contrary to the Word of God. In the Lord's assignment to me of The Clarion Call, I find myself sharing the Word of God while encouraging and uplifting people wherever I go.

*Chapter 4*

# ALLOW GOD TO USE YOU

God desires to use you as an instrument of His Will. Once we are saved, we must receive Jesus as our Lord, not just our Savior. Receiving Jesus as Lord means we fully surrender our decisions and plans to Him and trust Him to lead us through this world. We must also receive the Baptism of the Holy Spirit and <u>allow</u> the Lord's

*OBEY TODAY!*
*Obedience only*
*works today.*

Spirit to lead us. This means consciously choosing, daily, to do God's Will, as He leads you, not your own will. We have the power of God's Holy Spirit living on the inside of us, guiding us. The same power that raised Jesus from the dead lives in us. We can "do all things (anything the Lord asks us to do) through Christ who strengthens us" (Phil. 4:13).

In the earth realm, the Lord has no hands but our hands. He has no voice in the earth realm but our voice. The Lord needs you to be an instrument of His Will to do His work in this world. The Lord needs your hands to do, your feet to go, and your mouth to speak as He Wills. He needs you to submit your will to Him and obey Him. He needs your voice to say the things He leads you to say. It is HIS Will and His purpose that must be done, not yours.

God could use a donkey if He wanted to, but He chooses you. No matter your level of spiritual maturity, whether you are a babe in Christ or a preacher of the Gospel, God can use you. You may wonder how God could use a babe in Christ. Just as a three-year-old toddler can help his mom by bringing her the brush to groom his new baby sister's hair, God can use you. You may be a babe in Christ, but if your heart is toward God, He can use you.

The more mature in the Word you become, and the closer your relationship with the Lord, the more He can and will use you. That toddler is now a mature, responsible teenager able to help mom by running errands to the store. The more you come out of the world, put down stubbornness and rebellion, learn how to control your flesh, pray, and daily guard your heart, the more God will use you. The more spiritually mature you become, the more the Lord will use you at an increasingly greater level of purpose. That teen is now a fully mature adult, president of a company, asking God to lead him in serving his employees and clients. The president is a servant leader who exemplifies being a credible witness through company values, policies, quality of product, service to customers, and treatment of his employees. The more you obey and trust the Lord, the greater the level of purpose the Lord will use you.

## WHEN IT DOESN'T MAKE SENSE (TO YOUR NATURAL MIND)

I offer a few personal experiences as examples of obeying the Lord when it did not make sense to my natural mind. In each scenario, the Lord was using me to be a blessing to someone else. The Lord was also teaching me, training me, strengthening me, and preparing me for greater tests, tasks, and trials to come.

## REPAIRER OF THE BREACH

During my morning devotion one day, I was reading Isaiah 58, and when I read verse 6, the Scripture began to flash at me. (That is just the way the Lord signals me when He wants something specific of me.) I knew I was to work with the Scripture and tangibly create something. I got a sheet of paper, turned it horizontally, and sketched what I saw: a line across the top, and one across the bottom, with two columns in the middle — one on the left, one on the right, and a vertical line between the two columns. That is all I "saw" to do that day. God was not "speaking" to me; I just felt led to do what I was doing. Each day, I would go back to that scripture with my paper. The two columns were to become words. Each day, I wrote another sentence, added another phrase. This went on for two weeks. Then I sensed that I was to replace the line across the top with a person's name: my pastor's name! Further, I was to add a title at the top: "The Repairer of the Breach." At this point, I got frantic! My pastor was to be re-ordained (since the church had pulled away from its former denomination). This "paper" was to represent the gratitude of the congregation and be presented to my pastor at his ordination service.

# Pastor John A. Cherry

## From The Heart Church Ministries

*Teach all who will listen,*

Loose the bands of wickedness,
Undo heavy burdens,
Let the oppressed go free, break every yoke.
Deal thy bread to the hungry,
Bring the poor that are cast out to thy house.
When thou seeth the naked, cover him;
Hide not thyself from thine own flesh.

Then shall thy light break forth as the morning,
Thine health shall spring forth speedily:
Thy righteousness shall go before thee:
The glory of the Lord shall be thy rereward.
Then shalt thou call and the Lord shall answer:
Thou shalt cry and he shall say, Here I am.

Take away from the midst of thee the yoke,
the putting forth of the finger and speaking vanity:
Draw out thy soul to the hungry,
Satisfy the afflicted soul.

Then shall thy light rise in obscurity,
And thy darkness be as the noon day:
The Lord shall guide thee continually, and
Satisfy thy soul in drought and make fat thy bones:
Thou shalt be like a watered garden,
Like a spring of water, whose waters fail not.
And they that shall be of thee shall build the old waste places

*Thou shalt raise up the foundations of many generations;*
*and thou shalt be called,*

# The Repairer of the Breach (ISA 58:6-12)

## To Commemorate Your Consecration

Wherefore also we pray always for you, that our God would count you worthy of this
calling, and fulfil all the good pleasure of his goodness, and the work of faith with
power: That the name of our Lord Jesus Christ may be glorified in you, and ye in him,
according to the grace of our God and the Lord Jesus Christ.

(2 Thes. 1:11-12)

*We Love You Pastor, Your Sheep*
*September 12, 1999*

I don't know if I was nervous, anxious, or excited; I just knew that at that point, I felt like this paper was a hot potato. I wanted to finish it and get it out of my hands. Then I felt led to replace the line across the bottom with a Scripture out of II Thessalonians that was a prayer for the pastor (II Thess. 1:11–12).

I phoned the church and spoke with someone who was coordinating the ordination. I told her of the project and that I thought this was something the Lord wanted presented to the pastor. I took her a draft copy. Every word on the "presentation" was Scripture. She liked it. I asked a graphic artist to design something to replace the line in the middle. She created a beautiful abstract image of Christ's head with a crown of thorns, and one drop of red blood running down the side of his face. She also designed the graphic layout of the entire presentation. I paid to have the presentation enlarged and framed; it was now a piece of art. I dropped it off at the church; the baton was now in someone else's hand. The framed work was presented to the pastor during the ordination, by a dedicated couple in the church, with love and appreciation from the entire congregation. Pastor Cherry was beaming during the presentation. It was a total surprise to him. I sat in the audience near the back during the presentation, humbled and grateful, thanking the Lord for using me to honor my pastor.

The Lord did not show me what I was creating, or why I was creating it, until the presentation was nearly finished. I was near the last step when I felt led to place the pastor's name at the top of the page. It was only then that I realized what I was creating. Sometimes, if we knew the end or outcome of what the Lord has us working on, we may get scared and feel incapable of carrying out such a big task. God does not explain to us; He leads us. We are to obey and trust. What if I had ignored God's prompting to do something with the Scripture when it flashed at me?

*God does not explain to us; He leads us.*

What if I did not go back to the paper every day for two weeks? What if I had not taken a draft copy of the presentation to the organizer? What if I had made up in my mind that the church would not accept the presentation because they were only a few days before the ordination service, and surely, they had finished planning the program? We must obey day by day, step by step as the Lord leads. It may not make sense to you now, but if you know the Lord is prompting you to do something, you must do it just as He said, and trust all will turn out for the good.

## FELICIA, MANDY, AND DIANE

Three times, the Lord has orchestrated for me to take someone into my home to live; each time occurred spontaneously with no prior notice or preparation. In each situation with Felicia, Mandy, and Diane (pseudo names), I did not know them previously; the Lord orchestrated bringing us together. And on each occasion, they and I knew it was the Lord.

Felicia and I attended the same church and knew each other as members, but we were not acquaintances. We spoke briefly once about her wanting to move, and I told Felicia about my family home as a possible option. Months later, I was leaving the church after service and had gone outside. Suddenly, I felt led to go back inside the building. I went inside not knowing what I was to do or where I was to go. I walked down the crowded hallway toward the ladies' room. Then I saw Felicia talking with two women. In passing, I quickly asked her if she had moved yet. She said no, but that she just knew she would have moved by now. In that instant, everyone around us seemed to disappear as if we were the only two people in what was a crowded hallway. Felicia said she had looked at a few places but had not found anywhere. I asked her if she had considered my family house, and she responded that she did not really want a whole house; she just needed a small place for herself and her daughter. I told her perhaps she could just use a couple of bedrooms in the family house. She began saying that could possibly work. But in the midst of her speaking, the Lord spoke to me, "That's not the house." So, as Felicia was beginning to comment, I said, "That's not the house." She looked at me, puzzled, asking, "That's not the house? Then which house?" The Lord said nothing. I told Felicia the only other house I could vouch for was my own. She looked at me intently and said, "Sister Liggins! Your heart!" Felicia and I did not know each other, except as members of the same church, so she was stunned that I would offer my home to her, on the spot. I was a bit surprised, myself. But that is was what the Lord led me to do.

I knew Felicia would need to see the house, so I asked if she were available on Thursday evening to come to my home. I chose Thursday for her to come by, just to buy some time. The house was already clean, but I knew I would need to show Felicia the whole house, and I wanted to ensure a couple of things were tidy. As Felicia was answering me about coming on Thursday, the Lord said, "Today." Again, as Felicia was beginning to answer, I said, "Felicia, it's today. Can you come today?" She said she was to have lunch with her daughter and girlfriend after church but should be able to be there by 4:00 pm. I drove all the way home praising the Lord! Four o'clock was perfect. I did not need to wait until Thursday; I just needed thirty minutes to tidy up a few things.

Felicia came by with her 14-year-old daughter to see the house. They loved it. We agreed on terms, and they moved in the first of the month. A couple days after they settled, Felicia came to me in grateful tears, thanking me for having them in my home. Felicia and her daughter had both been tempted of the flesh where they lived. She said she felt "safe" for the first time in a long time. We both thanked God. She was thankful to have somewhere safe and wholesome to live. I was thankful the Lord used me to answer Felicia's prayer.

Mandy. I met Mandy through a delegation of entrepreneurs traveling from Cameroon, Africa, to the USA. Each entrepreneur was paired with an American entrepreneur for housing. The coordinator phoned me one evening saying they were short of host homes and needed to place three people. He asked if I would host. I agreed and asked him when they would arrive, and he said the next day. I hesitated, he pleaded, and I agreed to host one of the delegates. An interpreter brought Mandy to my home the next day for a two-week stay. Mandy spoke French and very little English. I spoke very slowly, and we managed to get along quite well.

When Mandy was not with the delegation, I toured her around town to introduce her to our American lifestyle. Simple things like the mail carrier delivering mail to my mailbox, trash picked up at the curb, and driving through a carwash all amazed Mandy. I took her grocery shopping so she could prepare a Cameroonian dinner. Mandy bragged about me so much to the other delegates that they became envious. Some of them simply had a room in a house but no meaningful interaction with the host homeowner. Mandy was a tailor and was exceptionally talented in her skill; her designs and seamstress handiwork were impeccable. I took her to fabric stores and explained how Americans match colors and how we don't wear plaids with flowers. She measured me but was so busy with her delegation there was no time to sew. At the end of her two-week visit with the delegation, we promised to stay in touch.

A month after returning home, Mandy sent me a package via the delegation organizer. It was a beautiful tailor-made business suit designed specifically for me. Mandy had measured me while living in my home, but she made the suit after she returned home to Cameroon, Africa, which meant NO fittings, yet the suit fit me perfectly! It remains one of my favorite suits.

Mandy was determined to get back to the United States. She moved to a slum area in Cameroon to save money so she could return.

We communicated via email, though Mandy's written English was difficult to interpret. I wrote a Letter of Invitation for Mandy to return to America, and God blessed Mandy to have her VISA approved. Out of fear of someone blocking her VISA, Mandy did not tell anyone in Cameroon about her desire to return to America, except Joe, another Cameroonian entrepreneur who served as our email translator. Even I did not know WHEN Mandy wanted to return. I knew within the month, but not exactly when. One morning, Joe emailed me that Mandy was in flight and would arrive at LaGuardia Airport in New York that day and would phone me for me to navigate her to Maryland! Mandy was arriving that day! I had no idea how to get from LaGuardia Airport in New York to Maryland. I went online and feverishly searched the Amtrak rail system between New York and Maryland. Fortunately, there is a station three miles from me.

Mandy spoke very little English, was at a huge airport in New York, had no transportation, and she did not know America's rail or bus system, nor her way around huge airports. She phoned me when she landed. I had Mandy give her cell phone to anyone walking near her though she did not know English enough to explain why she was giving them the phone. To whomever took her phone, I explained our challenge and that I wanted to get Mandy from where she was at that point to the Amtrak train. The Lord blessed five different people to take time to stop and take Mandy's phone for me to explain the next step. The Lord navigated Mandy through the help of kind strangers, step by step through LaGuardia Airport, then to the shuttle to take her to the Amtrak Station, then to the exact train that would get Mandy to Maryland. I purchased a ticket online for Mandy. I spoke with the Amtrak conductor and pleaded with him to watch for Mandy to ensure she got off at the right stop in Maryland.

I was to meet Mandy at the New Carrollton Amtrak Station. It was mid-December at 8:00 PM, so temperatures had dropped; it was freezing cold. I waited on the platform as everyone got off the train.

No Mandy. I waited. The train was emptying. Then I saw at the far end, near the conductor, a woman emerging with several bags of luggage. I knew it was Mandy. I ran to her yelling her name to let her know it was me. Mandy had just left Africa where the temperature was 90 degrees. She had on a white gauze Summer dress with flip-flop shoes, toes wide open. She did have on a sweater she had packed. She also had on a neck scarf — a gift from a kind stranger at the New York airport who had compassion for her, recognizing from her clothing that she was not from this country and was not prepared for the freezing cold. I pulled off my coat and gave it to her. Mandy had made it back to America!

Diane. In pursuing government contract work, I began interviewing candidates for a position, should the contract come through. I posted a notice at my church. A member told Diane of the position opening and referred Diane to me. Diane phoned. She said she was not a member of my church, but she was a member of the Body of Christ. We met for the interview, and she had just the skills I needed. However, I wanted to hire someone from my church.

It was April. The contract slowed, so I slowed the interviewing. Over the next couple of months, I asked the Lord why Diane was so heavy on my heart. I knew there were members of my church who could use the job, but I did not understand why Diane was so heavy on my heart.

In June, the contract solicitation picked back up, so I reached out to Diane for a second interview. She was surprised, thinking I had already hired someone else. When we met for the interview, while still standing up Diane started saying, "I really wanted to work with you. I really wanted to work for your company. But so much has happened since our first interview. So much has happened since we scheduled THIS interview." I wondered why she was standing up, and why she was speaking in past-tense. Then Diane sat down and started sharing. (Diane later told me the Lord said to tell me everything.) She began to pour out her story to me. Diane had six children by four fathers. The father of her youngest two girls married her but left, (he said later) because Diane refused to work. After the husband left, Diane was evicted from the apartment. She split her children up, keeping three with her. Her oldest son, in his early twenties, went with his father, a preacher. The two youngest girls went to stay with their dad, her husband. As a Veteran, Diane could get housing weekly at Andrews AFB and Bolling AFB. So, every week, Diane and the three remaining children bounced from Andrews, to Bolling to motels. When school ended in May, the three children were sent to New York for the summer to stay with their grandmother. Diane continued to bounce from Andrews to Bolling to motels.

On the day of our second interview, Diane was to have checked out of the motel. However, she forgot to notify her oldest son, who was to help her lift her heavy duffle bags. By the time she reached her son and he arrived, they were both frazzled. Her son insisted that she stop bouncing from place to place and go to New York to stay with her mother. The son told Diane he was taking her to the train station, right then and there! Diane told him of our interview and that I was already at the hotel waiting. The son dropped her off and told her to go in and just tell the lady (me) that she could not take the job because she had to move to New York. Meanwhile, the son sat in the car waiting. That is why Diane started her conversation in past-tense, saying she really wanted to work with me. During the discussion, Diane looked perplexed and said to me, "My son is a minister, and I know he thinks he has the plan of God for our lives, but I just don't believe I'm supposed to go to New York."

The whole time Diane was speaking, the Lord was moving on my heart. I had asked the Lord in April why Diane was so heavy on my heart when I knew there were members of my church who could use the job. Since April, He had not answered. Now, when Diane began pouring out her story to me, the Lord said, "That's why she was so heavy on your heart."

When Diane said she didn't think she was to go to New York, I told her, "The job is yours if the contract comes through. And I have a place you can lay your head, if you'd like." Diane was shocked. She said, "You mean I can live with you?" I said, "If you'd like." Diane said, "Today? My son is ready to take me to the train station now!" I said, "If you'd like." Diane was thrilled.

Just then, Diane's son walked into the lobby where we were sitting. He had a bright face and a warm smile. Diane went to him to share her good news. As Diane spoke, the son's face turned from bright and warm to angry and ugly; he stormed out the door. Diane followed him outside. I gathered my things and went outside and approached the son. I was glad Diane mentioned that he was a minister. I said to her son, "I know you did not come here thinking your mother would be leaving with some stranger. I did not come here thinking some stranger would be coming to my home. I know you don't know me, but I am your sister in Christ. I do know how to hear from the Lord, and when I hear, I obey." I could SEE the anger dissipate from his face. I could see the Lord moving on his heart. I gave the son my address and phone number. I invited him to follow me to my home so he would know where his mother would be and that she was not staying with some crazy lady.

Diane rode with her son to my home. They came in, and he carried her heavy duffle bags to her room. We sat at the kitchen table for two hours as I shared my story and how the Lord has worked in my life. Afterward, the son, who is a minister, simply said to me, "You have an awesome walk."

That was June. In August, Diane's three children in New York were calling and asking when they were coming back to Maryland to get ready for school. Diane had told me that the three children in New York were a boy, 17 years old, and two girls, 15 and 10 years old. The contract I was pursuing did not come through, so I was not able to hire Diane. She worked for my company anyway, to offset her living expenses. Diane would daily go online looking for apartments; however, with no salary, an apartment was out of reach. She kept looking, trying to find someplace to house her family. After a couple of weeks, I could see the frustration mounting in Diane. I told Diane to have the children move here, as well. She cried and thanked me.

Then the devil said, "Didn't she tell you she had a 17-year-old son? You know, pants hanging down the butt, 'Yo bro, what's up' 17-year-old? And, didn't she say she had a 15-year-old girl? A sassy, prissy 15-year-old? And, when was the last time you were around a 10-year-old?" I did not address the devil.

I said to the Lord, "Father, You told me to let them come. I trust You."

All three of Diane's children were wonderful, well behaved, mannerly, friendly, and clean. They were happy to be in a home and were comfortable here. The son was awesome and the friendliest. He immediately became a little brother to my son; they went fishing and camping together.

I was thankful for the opportunity for the Lord to use me to bless Diane's family by sharing the blessings the Lord had given me through my home.

On each occasion with Felicia, Mandy, and Diane, the Lord orchestrated them coming to live in my home at a time of their crisis. In each scenario, they and I knew the Lord brought them to my home. In each scenario, we all were praising the Lord.

## Mrs. B., My Neighbor

Mrs. B was my neighbor who lived directly across the street from me. I met Mrs. B. through a phone call. She phoned me one day introducing herself, saying that she was blind, so she visited neighbors by phone. Mrs. B. learned of me through her husband who walked their dog daily. Mr. B. loved to talk. We would often have long talks out by the mailbox about his parents' journey from Italy, his wife and children, and his work before retirement. He told me that they had lost two of their three children. One as a baby boy born with severe birth defects caused by prescription drugs given to his wife during her pregnancy. The second son was an avid swimmer who, at 17 years old, drowned. It was a difficult period for Mr. and Mrs. B. and their daughter. It was nearly devastating for Mrs. B; she blamed God for both of her sons' deaths. I knew all of this before Mrs. B. ever reached out to introduce herself to me by phone.

Mr. and Mrs. B. were an Italian Catholic couple who lived with their daughter and son-in-law. They were a wonderful couple. Mrs. B. would phone me every two weeks or so, to "visit." We talked about any and everything, sometimes for well over an hour. I was working from home, but I felt led to take the time to talk with Mrs. B. She would often say things that I knew were outside the Word of God, and I would gently state the truth, and we would keep going. I would not let Mrs. B. get by with saying anything that was not in line with the Word. In the early stages of our hour-long phone visits, if Mrs. B said something that conflicted with the Word, I would lovingly let her have it and simply state truth. Mrs. B. would say, "Well, I have to go take my medicine." As we would hang up, I thought, Lord, she'll never call me again!

About two weeks later, Mrs. B. would call. We would have a wonderful hour or two conversation. I'd speak truth when correction was necessary, she'd have to go take her medicine, and two weeks later, she'd call again. I knew the Lord was using me to minister to Mrs. B.

While on the phone one day, we were talking about the loss of her sons. Mrs. B. was still hurting about the loss and was angry with God about it. I told her she needed to let the anger go; to ask the Lord to help her let the anger go. Mrs. B. said, "Before you can ask God anything, you have to first believe there is a God. As far as I am concerned, all you have to do is be nice. You are nice; you could be my god! Arthur (another neighbor) is nice; he could be my god!" Mrs. B. was really hurting, and only love and the Lord would bring her through.

Then one day, Mrs. B. invited me over for tea and crumpets. I would always accept her invitation, no matter how busy I was. I had a wonderful in-person visit with Mr. and Mrs. B., every time. At least once per month, Mrs. B would invite me over for tea. Mrs. B was blind, but she had sight until she was about 50 years old, so she could envision what things looked like. She would go to a wedding and then describe to me how beautiful the bride's dress was. Someone would describe the dress to Mrs. B., and she could envision it enough to describe it to me, in detail. Mrs. B. considered herself a jogger. She did 1,000 "jogs" every day. She would hold on to the back of a chair and run in place: 300 jogs after breakfast, 300 after lunch, and 400 after dinner. Mrs. B. was a real delight.

The phone visits, along with tea and crumpets, went on for over 10 years. My loving chastisement went along with it, in every conversation. Both Mr. and Mrs. B. were in their 80s. Mr. B. had already confessed Jesus as Lord. During one phone visit, I told Mrs. B. that I wanted her in Heaven with me, that we were all going to die and there were only two options: Heaven or Hell. I told her that now, on earth, is when we choose where we have eternal life.

Over the years, on three separate occasions in the middle of the night, the roaring engine of an ambulance would awaken me. I would start praying, "Not yet, Lord. Please! She's not ready." The next day, the daughter would tell me it was just a scare, and her mom was alright.

One day during our phone visit, Mrs. B. said, "I was talking to the Lord and I asked Him [this, or that]." My heart was overjoyed! For Mrs. B. to go from telling me that I could be her god, to her praying to our Heavenly Father, just blessed my heart!

Then, one day, Mrs. B. had a fall while in their bedroom. She broke her shoulder and her hip, and the trauma of the breaks gave her a heart attack. I went to the hospital to see her. Her daughter and a friend were there. I went over to Mrs. B. and stroked her forehead, calling her name and telling her that I was there. Mrs. B. began to move as if to desperately try to open her eyes. Her daughter had not seen that kind of movement before. With a hip and shoulder break, Mrs. B. was heavily sedated, so much that no matter how hard she tried, she could not open her eyes. I held her hand and told her that it was okay and just to rest.

Mrs. B. died in the hospital. Though I was sorry to see her go, I actually felt joy at Mrs. B.'s passing. I was joyful only because she had accepted Jesus as Lord and Savior! All the years of ministering through friendship were blessings in disguise, for both of us. It was time well spent. I trusted that Mrs. B. was already in Heaven. I thanked the Lord for my 10-year assignment with Mrs. B.; it was a wonderful journey together. Mrs. B. was truly a delight.

## Ten Alligators Nipping at My Heels

I went through periods where multiple major trials were occurring in my life, and all were in operation concurrently. Each major challenge was enough on its own to knock me off my feet. I felt like I was like Peter walking on the water, looking at Jesus. But while walking on the water, I had ten alligators nipping at my heels. Each alligator represented a different, yet concurrent trial. I remembered that Peter sank when he took his eyes off Jesus and focused on his circumstances. I did not want to sink; I knew I could not focus on my circumstances. I could not focus on the ten alligator trials that were nipping at me. It was nearly overwhelming. I knew these trials were a test of my faith. All I could do was to draw myself away from the world; away from TV, activities, and people. I needed to cocoon myself in the Word and in the love of the Lord. I knew I had to be steadfast, seek the Lord, obey His directions, and trust God. Jesus was my only hope.

Two seasons of my ten alligator trials:

**1991–2002.** 1991 was a great year for me. I had been a business development consultant to a federal government contractor. I brought this company 37 million dollars in federal contracts in two years. The president was so impressed that he asked me to come on board full-time. I initially scoffed at his offer, but then spiritually felt it was what I should do. The economy was in recession. New contracts were rare. He made me an offer I felt led to take. He asked me to give him only one year. I required two things of him: 1) I report directly to him, the president, and 2) do not clip my wings. I had supported his company for two years as a consultant, so he was accustomed to my work ethic and my judgment. He agreed.

A few years later, I was still there, enjoying the independence of an entrepreneur with none of the risks. As my employer, the company became a sponsor in the 1995 Special Olympic World Games held in New Haven, Connecticut. The Special Olympics follows the same organizational pattern as the World Olympics; 144 countries were participating in over 70 athletic categories. I was the corporate coordinator to oversee the company's sponsorship role in the Games to include publicity, hotel, travel, staffing, and guest participation, along with gold, silver, and bronze medal award presentations for our venue. The Games were a great occasion and an endearing experience. Everything went flawlessly, except I had to "save the president's neck" from a major snafu with one of the larger corporate sponsors for the World Games. The president gave me a twenty-thousand-dollar raise for my efforts.

Also, in 1995, at my church, Full Gospel, I took a class called "The Seven Spiritual Principles." The class was awesome; it took me on a life-changing journey of spiritual growth. Also, for the church, I supported the planning and implementation of a major church convention attended by hundreds of leaders and visiting pastors. The convention was hosted by Pastor John A. Cherry, who after teaching a message at one of the sessions, gave a call to Christ. I was amazed at his boldness to give a call to Christ with the ballroom filled with other pastors and their leaders. Men came forward and filled the altar, wall-to-wall, to give or rededicate their lives to Christ. I loved the boldness of my pastor in obeying the Lord, no matter what the Lord led him to do.

Additionally, in 1995, my sisters and I honored our mom's 73rd birthday with a black-tie gala. The theme was "The Life and Legacy of a Virtuous Woman." Some people thought we should wait until our mom was 75 years old for such a big event, but the siblings decided to honor our mom then with the gala and do something even better when she turned 75. My mother was elated! The event was a total surprise to my mom for her November birthday. We had all her friends, family, and church members attend. Each daughter gave tribute to our mom, giving her flowers while she could see them. Mom later told us that if we did nothing else in life for her, she was satisfied.

Three months after the gala for my mother, February 1996, doctors diagnosed my mother with pancreatic cancer. At the time of diagnosis, the doctor also told her that it was terminal. She was told she had about five months to live and would likely not live past July.

During this same period in early 1996, one of my sisters, Jackie, was battling an illness caused by a botched surgery where the doctor unknowingly punctured her intestine several years earlier. Jackie's body went into shock a few hours after surgery. They said some type of bacteria was invading her body. Doctors pumped her with every type antibiotic they could think of; such that she became so bloated, that even in a coma, her eyeballs became swollen to the point that her eyelids would not close. They told us she had a twenty percent chance of living. And if Jackie did live, she would have a soggy brain with the mind of a twelve-year-old. Weeks passed before they discovered that bile from the punctured intestine was the source of the infection. Doctors changed the antibiotic and a few weeks later, Jackie came out of the coma. Unfortunately, during those several weeks before addressing the punctured intestine, the leaked bile caused so much damage that her intestinal tissue and stomach tissue were too thin and weak to stitch back together. Surgeons literally could not stitch her intestine together. Whenever she ate food, it poured right out of her open stomach. Jackie had to have a plastic bag glued to her stomach to catch the food and pump it into a holding tank. Food that Jackie ate did her good emotionally — we are wired to get hunger pangs and to eat — but the food Jackie ate did her no physical good; it poured right out of her stomach into the plastic bag. Jackie's body had lost the ability to digest and process food. She had to be fed intravenously; not through a vein but through an artery. To get a port into Jackie's artery required surgery. Our arteries are not designed to carry food for any length of time. Each artery would wear out after three months or so and the port would be relocated to a different part of her body. This meant surgery every three months. Jackie lived half of her last five years in the hospital going through surgery and fighting infections. Ultimately, doctors ran out of fresh arteries to place the port. Jackie also had a major infection. Doctors told Jackie she wouldn't live past July 1996.

This meant that both my mother and my sister were on their deathbed at the same time, both with life expectancies that ran out in July 1996. We did not know which one was going to die first, literally. Fortunately, Jackie's husband, Ronald, took exceedingly great around-the-clock care of Jackie. For my mother, five of her daughters created a twenty-four-hour rotation schedule of care rotating days of the week and rotating weekends. The five of us went to a four-day workweek so we could each take a 24-hour rotation to care for Mom.

In May of 1996, one of our cousins passed, and we all went to the funeral. Both Jackie and Mom were able to attend, both in wheelchairs. They had not seen each other for a while since they both had been in and out of hospitals. At my cousin's funeral, we rolled Jackie's and Mom's chairs side by side, facing each other. Jackie and Mom hugged each other and cried. They both would have gladly given their life for the sake of the other. But they were both dying, and they both knew they were dying.

During all this, also in 1996, my baby sister, Cricket, announced she was pregnant. This was great news because she and her husband had wanted a baby for eight years. Cricket had undergone a partial hysterectomy and had only one-half of an ovary left. We were all excited about Cricket's pregnancy. We normally would have showered Cricket with loads of fun and attention. After all, Cricket was the baby of the family, and we always spoiled her rotten. Now it was different. We were all laden with the burden of knowing our mother and sister were dying. It was emotionally draining on all of us. It was particularly emotionally draining on Cricket, who was both elated with her own good news but depressed with the lingering terminal illness of our mother and sister.

Jackie died at the end of August; her funeral was September 3. Cricket's birthday was September 7th. Her baby was born September 14. It was a real emotional roller-coaster for all of us, but especially for Cricket.

Mom was home the day Jackie died, but the news of Jackie's death sent Mom to the hospital to intensive care. I spent the night with Mom in intensive care the night before Jackie's funeral. I washed her hair and did her nails; that was my regular mother-daughter bonding regimen. I used the hospital shower and got dressed for Jackie's funeral. The doctors came in and told Mom she could not go to the funeral; it was too great of a risk for her heart. Mom softly but firmly told the doctors, "I am going to my daughter's funeral." After much back and forth from the doctors, they realized they would not be able to stop my mother from leaving. They insisted she sign a release form; she said fine. They insisted she go by ambulance; she said fine. They insisted she keep on the oxygen tube; she said fine. They insisted she stay on the gurney the entire time; she said fine.

After all the time spent back and forth with the doctors, we were late for the funeral. I phoned ahead to let my older sister know what was going on at the hospital. She informed the pastor. My mother was mother of the church, and everyone in the church loved my mom and

Jackie. The pastor held up the funeral, waiting on the mother of the church to arrive. When the ambulance pulled up to the church with my mom, the doors of the church swung open and the choir began to sing. The attendants rolled Mom into the church on the gurney with the back propped up to seat her upright. The church erupted in cheers and praise when they saw Mom! They were not going to start that funeral without Mom, the mother of the church! Jackie had a wonderful home-going service. She was a gentle, kind-hearted person. Everyone who knew her loved her. Jackie was my favorite sister and best friend.

My dad had been my best friend; he passed in 1989. Now, my next best friend, Jackie, was gone. I wondered why the Lord would take the only two people who really knew me, who really understood me. In some ways, I believe it is partly because He wanted me to depend on Him, and Him alone, for friendship and advice. I began to do just that.

By October, Mom's doctors were telling us they did not understand why she was still alive since they had thought she wouldn't live past July. They said she had defied every rule in the book regarding life expectancy with her condition. Mom's doctor loved our family; he loved how we cared for Mom. Her doctor knew we did not want to put Mom in hospice care or even a nursing home. Mom stayed in the hospital, getting radiation and chemotherapy, even when it was evident that no form of treatment was getting her any better. Mom signed a do-not-resuscitate order (DNR). She was the last of a family of 13 children. Mom was the matriarch of the family. She had helped to plan many, many funerals. She had seen many people on life support, delaying the inevitable. Mom knew her cancer was terminal and did not want a machine keeping her alive. The DNR sometimes made it difficult for us, because as her children, the moment we saw something going wrong for her, our first reaction was to want the doctors to jump in and fix it. However, with the DNR, the doctors' only orders were to keep Mom comfortable. We had to keep reminding ourselves, this is what Mom wanted.

Mom died on New Year's Eve, 1996. We all gathered at the hospital in her private room. We sang Gospel songs, prayed, and praised the Lord. It was just like Mom to bring the matter to a close at the close of the year. I believe the Lord allowed Mom a little extra time, from July to December, to release anger she felt toward one of her earlier doctors. She had told that doctor for years that she felt something was wrong. He would only tell her she needed to lose weight. By the time that doctor took Mom seriously, she was already terminal. She was angry about that. I believe God in His mercy and grace, knew Mom loved Him and allowed her time to be at peace in her heart before calling Mom home to be with Him. Mom's home-going service was in early January 1997. I wanted to regroup from the multiple traumas of 1996. I took the whole month of January 1997 off from work.

In early 1996 at work, I received a promotion to associate director for Business Development & Client Relations. The president of the company had relied on my judgment regularly since 1991. I had been the president's sounding board, his first advisor, the person he would go to when he had a new idea and wanted to strategize the best ways to implement the idea. That all changed starting April of '96 when I went to a four-day workweek to care for Mom. I went to work four days a week, but I wasn't really there. The challenges of losing my sister and mother were taking their toll. At work, I had downshifted; I was not on my toes and not as much in the game. I could see during this time that others were trying to get the president's ear, and I did not care. For seven years, they had envied my role of having the president's ear, and they were obvious in their clamoring to gain that role. They knew I had downshifted and was not fully engaged; this was their time to jockey for my position. I felt sorry for them clamoring to gain the president's ear, to get that position of trust. I felt sorry for them because with all that was going on with my family in 1996 with Cricket, Jackie, and Mom, the work, the president, and the company seemed much less relevant to me. The work environment began to feel worldly.

It is interesting how the Lord shows you things you do not expect to see. During this same time, the Lord showed me a vision of how to take what I had done over seven years at that one company and create a business entity to provide those same services to multiple companies. I had been a consultant previously, which is how I met the president of this company. Now, seven years later, the Lord was showing me a vision for a new thing. I was to take all that the Lord showed me in how to support this one company and to start my own business to serve other companies as well. The president got very angry with me when I told him I was leaving. I told him this was something I must do, that I was led to do and that I wanted him to be happy for me, to support me. In October 1997, I launched Corporate Resource Solutions. This president became my first customer, wanting me to continue to provide services. It was clear to me that this business was an assignment from the Lord.

When the Lord wants to move you from one assignment to another, He will close the door on what you were doing so you cannot continue, and He will make it such that you will not want to continue the original work. Though my former employer became my first customer and signed a one-year contract when I started my business, I could not finish that contract year. I had no desire to support him or his company. What I had seen during 1996 when I downshifted showed me a company I could no longer serve. Fortunately, other companies were waiting for me to start my own business so I could provide business development services to them. I was thankful for them and thankful the Lord sent them to me.

> *There is always something good in every bad situation. No matter how bad the bad is, look for the good and focus on that. It will keep you.*

No matter how bad the situation or challenges may be, in the midst of the bad, there will always be something good. Search for the good; focus on the good. The good that you find amid a bad situation is the light that will keep your head lifted. It will keep your attitude positive and your heart right. While my co-workers were trying to lobby to gain the ear of the president, that same president was diminishing in relevance to me. The Lord was showing me an entirely new vision and a new direction He wanted me to take.

## THE WILDERNESS EXPERIENCE

When the Lord gives you a new assignment, there will always be a "wilderness experience," a period when the Lord will prepare you for the assignment. It will be a period of uncertainty, a period of testing your commitment to the assignment and your trust in the Lord.

After starting Corporate Resource Solutions (CORE), I went through a period where ninety percent of my time was doing ministry work at my church. I could not understand why I was not putting more time into building the business. I cried out to the Lord to tell me why I felt compelled to work the ministry even though I knew He wanted me to build the business. The Lord told me, "This is your training ground." I took the Perfecting Class at my church for the second time. The Perfecting Class teaches members to identify their functional spiritual gifts. I perceived from the teaching of this class that I had the gift of leadership. I was a leader; this was a new concept to me even though I had already served as lead on three ministry projects: 1) I had led the Marketing Team for the church's new credit union, 2) I had led the web support team recommending design of a new ministry website, and 3) I had coordinated a full-scale Christmas Gift Galleria

*The wilderness experience serves as your training ground.*

(a shopping mall open for eight weeks with more than fifty vendors). I did not recognize it at the time, but all the ministry activities were grooming me to become stronger in my areas of weakness. I had never considered myself a leader, even though I became a supervisor at 26 years old and a regional manager at 32. I mentioned to my oldest sister that I had never considered myself a leader and she replied, "I don't know why not!" How can one run a business and not recognize their leadership ability? Of all the positions I had ever held, organizing the three ministry functions pointed out my leadership qualities.

Immediately upon completion of the three projects in the ministry, the Lord released me to move forward with the business. I had learned from my "training ground," my wilderness experience, that I am a leader. As a leader in this business, I was to be the servant of all. The Lord began to send clients. CORE was to be a business; I was to no longer function as a consultant.

CORE did very well from 1997 until 2010. **2010 was tumultuous, yet beautiful** because I focused on that one positive thing. There is always something good in every bad situation. Look for the good and focus on that. My test of the 2010 trials follows.

I had two contractual business endeavors that went awry, devastating my financial base. I identified government contract opportunities that were set aside for a certified minority small business. My firm did not have the certification, so I brought in a business colleague who had the certification to be the prime contractor, with my firm as the subcontractor. Since I was the one who had a relationship with the government decision-maker, I introduced the new prime contractor to my government contact. On each subcontract arrangement, both companies I brought to the table ended up giving me the short end of the stick. A female president took advantage of nearly ten percent more monies for herself that should have come to my company and refused to rectify the matter. Further, she refused to listen to my recommendation that we take a different approach to serving the client. The client had turned down two of the prime's recommendations. When the third proposed recommendation was presented, the client was again very dissatisfied and chastised the prime mercilessly. The client then asked if I had any suggestions. I pulled out the presentation I had offered to the prime and made that presentation to the client. The client loved my approach and excitedly offered, on the spot, to fund my recommendation. As we were departing, the chastised prime told me, rather begrudgingly, "It was your heart." I still have good relations with that government contact.

The second prime-contractor incident in 2010 was more egregious. I brought in a male president into a four-year contract as the prime contractor since he had the requisite certifications; my company would be subcontractor. Soon after the contract started, his greed was evident. He spoke of another of his contracts and how he hated signing paychecks. He would regularly say, "I hate payday! I hate signing checks!" I tried to tell him he needed those employees to generate his current revenue. I began to recognize that if he hated signing small paychecks, he would not at all like signing over 49% of each of his contract revenue payments to me. Indeed, at the end of the first year of our four-year contract, the prime sent me a letter of termination, by certified mail. No discussion. I was devastated. I had six employees on this contract: four at the government site and two at my office. He told those who worked on-site at the government that they now worked for him, or they could quit. Two of them called me, huddled together in the stairwell, scared, whispering, and concerned for me. I told them I would be OK and that I was glad they still had their job. I was thankful to have hired them, as they were both unemployed prior to my bringing them on staff. I asked them to do their best, to continue to represent God, and to maintain their integrity as a CORE hire. The three of my hires were so good that later when the prime tried to fire them in fear of their loyalty to me, the government decision-maker instructed the prime to keep them.

With the loss of two of my largest federal contracts, my corporate revenue hit rock bottom. I knew it would take a while to rebuild, yet I held on to the two employees working at my office. I wanted them to remain employed, and I knew they could be of assistance on other projects. I had heard of a program where, in financial difficulties, you could get your mortgage restructured and have payments reduced significantly; that would be a great help. I had my assistant working feverishly to assist me in pulling the paperwork together. After weeks of organizing and preparation, I went to a regional gathering of lenders, bankers, and mortgage companies seeking to get my mortgage modification. My mortgage underwriter was present, and I met with them onsite at the event, reviewed my case with them, and got approval from the underwriter on the spot for the modification. I was thrilled. I later supplied all the material and the approval from the underwriter to my credit union. My credit union denied my application for modification because I was still current on my mortgage. I told them of my recent financial position and that I was trying to ward off falling behind on my mortgage. Nothing I told them helped. The underwriter approval was ignored.

Also, in 2010, I applied for Small Business Administration (SBA) 8a Certification for my company, CORE, so that I could pursue contracts on my own. I'd had enough of unscrupulous prime contractors. For five years, since 2005, I had managed a contract at The United States Agency for International Development (USAID), for one of my client companies. The client had just won a contract and the president asked me to attend a post-award meeting with him. At the post-award meeting, the government contracting officer insisted to the president that he assign me as the program manager on the contract. I was able to work the program manager role because it only required about 20 hours per month. The government officials loved my management approach. The employees were happy. The contract specialists they served were happy.

In 2010, when that client company's 5-year contract was over, the company could not pursue the contract as the prime contractor again because the company had grown out of the SBA 8a size standard. The government decision-makers wanted me to continue to support their work. I applied for the SBA 8a certification. After years of working on federal proposals, I was able to complete the SBA 8a application myself. I wanted to ensure that all required materials were incorporated, accurate, and organized. In my cover letter, I requested an expedited review of my application since I had a government official at USAID who wanted to award a contract to my company. Expedited reviews were allowed only if the applicant had a pending contract award. I did. However, for some reason, the reviewer of my application was not impressed. He toyed with me and my application for months, asking for everything and anything outside of what the application requested. No matter what I said, or submitted, the reviewer would ask for more. This meant weeks of additional administrative preparation and gathering of materials to ship off to the reviewer.

USAID postponed the decision to make the award, which gave me a little more time to get my certification. When I would speak with the SBA reviewer over the phone, I told him of my work at USAID; I told him how pleased they were with my management style. I told him I had supported 8a companies for years and could be the poster child for SBA. He would chuckle at my frustration. SBA denied my application and suggested I could appeal. I appealed. They denied my application again and said I had exhausted my appeal, so I would have to wait one year to reapply. I was devastated.

I attended the Congressional Black Caucus convention that year, and for the first time, I went into their exhibitor hall. The first exhibitor booth was from the White House. That intrigued me, so I approached the booth. Immediately, I began to tell the story of what took place with the SBA. The man strongly urged me to write up my situation and submit it to the White House because the Obama Administration was reviewing the SBA in incidents like mine. I am a fighter, but by this time, I had no fight left.

**I felt like I had been in the boxing ring and, after a 1-2-3 punch, I was down for the count.** Losing the two government contracts causing financial chaos, not getting the support of my credit union for the restructuring of my mortgage, not getting approval of my SBA certification, and then losing the opportunity to continue supporting the USAID contract were nearly overwhelming.

I poured myself into the Word, reading, fasting, praying, and praising the Lord. I was determined to keep my eyes on Jesus. I asked the Lord to show me what He wanted me to know, to do, and to learn. I asked Him to show me myself and where I needed to change. I asked Him to search my mind, and my heart, and to remove anything that did not please Him. I separated myself: no friends, no TV. In fasting, I gave up meat, starches, snacks, and sweets. In that one year, 2010, I did the 21-day Daniel fast four times. I needed comfort. I needed clarity. I needed direction.

## LOOK FOR THE GOOD

**Another endeavor had my attention in 2010.** A couple of years earlier in 2008, I began to notice the unflattering general behavior, appearance, and attitude of many young black boys and black men.

*There is always something good in the midst of every bad situation. Look for the good.*

In a State of Perception

I sensed that something was wrong regarding men in the African American community, but I had no idea what it was. I was in a state of perception like never before. Also in 2008, a friend who was a fellow in Leadership

Maryland encouraged me to apply for Leadership Maryland as well. I brushed it off, not taking it seriously. By 2009, my sensing that something was wrong was even stronger when looking at the landscape of black boys and men. I knew something was wrong, very wrong in the community. I did not know what it was, but I knew it was pervasive. In 2009, another friend who was also a fellow encouraged me to apply to Leadership Maryland. This time, I felt led to do so, and I applied. I became a fellow in the Leadership Maryland Class of 2010.

Each year, Leadership Maryland (LMD) brings together 52 leaders from around the state. Through a 10-month program, LMD introduces the leaders to the issues, challenges, opportunities, and resources around the state. Leaders in my class included participants such as the Maryland secretary of Labor, the administrator for Maryland Motor Vehicle Administration, the Governor's special secretary for Minority Affairs, and the commanding officer of Patuxent Naval Air Force Base. Many members of my class were participating in LMD to build their network; I sensed that I was on a spiritual journey. During our orientation session, to help us get to know each other, the facilitator asked each of us to tell something about ourselves that no one in the room knew. Some said funny things, where they wanted to travel, or what happened as a child. When the facilitator came to me, I had not thought of what I was going to say. The gift of exhortation is one of my spiritual functional gifts listed in Romans 12:6–8. An exhorter

*I love to be led by the Holy Spirit! It's always an adventure!*

opens his/her mouth and expects the Lord to speak. When the facilitator asked me to tell the class something about myself that no one knew, I answered saying, "I love to be led by the Holy Spirit!"

OK, so, I did not know what I was going to say, but I certainly did not expect to say that! This was not a church congregation. I did not know these people! This was our first day together. However, I did not cringe nor hesitate. I knew if it came out, that was what the Lord wanted me to say. In my heart, I said, "OK, Lord, we're on!" The facilitator asked, "So you love to be led by the Holy Spirit; and, why is that?" I answered, "Because it's always an adventure!" That is when I knew for sure that this was going to be a spiritual journey for me. I expected my classmates to shun me or at least to shy away from me, but they were fine.

Each month, all 52 classmates packed our bags and were off to a two-and-a-half-day training exercise in various regions of the state, exploring and being exposed to issues and resources. Everywhere we traveled, I saw something that confirmed my sensing that something was wrong in the black community. And everywhere I went, I saw resources I could tap.

In July of 2010, my Leadership Maryland class traveled to Cumberland, Maryland, to visit a maximum-security state prison. I learned that an inmate goes to a maximum-security prison only when their sentence is twenty years or more. One of the prison officials met LMD at our hotel and rode the bus with us from the hotel to the prison. He touted that the prison was a brand-new state-of-the-art facility. Our facilitator benignly told us that we would see a disparity in the makeup of staff and the residents. They were both right. The facility was brand new, with very shiny razor wire. There was an immense disparity in the staff population and the inmates. At least eighty percent of the inmates were black, while 100 percent of the officers were white.

I had never visited a prison, nor jail. I did not know the difference between a jail and a prison, nor could I have told you where one was located. In 2010, I was very proud of that! I was proud that I did not know the difference between a jail and a prison because that meant "that world does not touch my world." I was proud that I did not know the difference, but pride is blinding! I was blind as a bat as to what was going on in my community, right under my nose. More on that later.

LMD organizers divided the 52 members of my class into small groups of six. Security officers were assigned to each small group to take the groups on a tour of the massive facility. We had an intimate tour. I was the only black in my small group of six. We passed inmates as they were escorted in or out of the prison. I spoke to each of four young men escorted past us as we toured; I was the only one in my small group who spoke to passing inmates. Each young man greeted me in return. Each inmate looked like young men in my neighborhood, my church, and my family; they did not look like monsters. We visited the intake room and saw the x-ray chair the men must sit on to ensure they are not "hiding" anything to bring into the prison. We saw the mess hall where they ate, with circular holes in the walls about four feet from the floor, with office windows all around the top of the walls. We learned that the windows were the stations where the officers kept watch while the inmates were eating. The circular holes were openings to inject tear gas into the room should a fight break out amongst the inmates. The food was set out cafeteria-style with trays of food that slid out from a four-inch high opening between the tray and a metal shield. The shield was in place so inmates could not see who was serving their food, and those behind the metal shield could not see who they were serving. This was a security measure to ensure those serving the food would not 'accidentally sneeze,' or do something worse to the food of a rival inmate.

We visited the command center where the officer had at least eight large monitors so he could see multiple locations at the same time. We saw the officer push buttons to open doors or close doors. We saw men going in and out of rooms, some escorted, some not. Every inmate I saw in those monitors was black. I told the officer that I wanted to go into one of the prison cells. He asked his superior if there were any empty cells. Cell number seven was empty. As we started toward the cell, the other five women in my small group said, "I want to go! I want to go!" I really did not want them to go into the cell with me. I was the only black in my small group of six; trust me, we were NOT having the same experience!

The six of us went into the prison cell. I told the officer to close the cell door. He said, "Are you sure ma'am?" I said, "Close the door." The moment I heard the clink of that cell door closing, my life changed! That prison visit produced the most riveting experience I had ever encountered; it changed the course of my life, instantly! I knew I had to do something.

We finished the day out at the prison and returned to our hotel. The prison visit had taken its toll; everyone went to his or her rooms; we did NOT have the usual social gathering. The next day, everyone tried to act like the day before had never happened.

*When I heard the clink of that cell door closing, my life changed!*

Our October training exercise allowed the opportunity for each class member who wanted to participate to pose a question to the class relative to any of the previous months' activities. We wrote questions on a large sticky paper that posted on the wall. The questions posed conference-style workshops, where participants could choose which workshop they wanted to participate. My question was "How did the prison visit impact you?" There were four workshops at 9 o'clock, four at 11:00, and four at 2:00. My question was one of the 9:00 workshops. Classmates were free to sit in on any one of the four workshops. Quite a few sat in on my "How did the prison visit impact you?" workshop. We were all deeply engaged in the conversation and had an in-depth weighty discussion. One of our male participants burst out crying, loudly, and profusely. That afternoon, at the end of all the workshops, the facilitator gathered the 52 classmates together in a circle for reflection on the day's discussions. The man in my 9:00 workshop burst into tears again, loudly and profusely. Everyone in the circle was either dabbing their eyes or holding their head down. It was a moving experience.

The experience of that day would not leave me. After we all returned home, I sent an email to all 52 of my classmates. I said to them, **"Whenever a discussion takes place that evokes an emotion in nearly every person in the room, we witness the genesis of an assignment — a clarion call to action."** The next day, my classmates flooded my email with "I accept the call! Sign me up." My classmates began to call the "project" The Clarion Call, which is how my current nonprofit organization got its name. It would take someone with a big head and a huge ego to start a nonprofit and name it The Clarion Call; the name alone implies a move of God. Moreover, because of my statement the very first day that we all met, "I love to be led by the Holy Spirit! It's always an adventure," and my conduct throughout the year, my classmates knew I was serious and was committed to moving forward with The Clarion Call. Toward the closing session for our class, everyone wrote reflections of their year-long experiences, identifying leaders and leadership styles that had inspired them throughout the year. We all received copies of the 52 class write-ups. I was immensely humbled to see my name referenced numerous times by at least half my classmates as a leader who inspired them.

Yes, the year 2010 was tumultuous yet beautiful. Even though I went

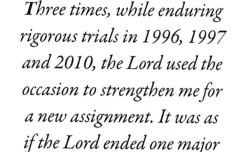

*Three times, while enduring rigorous trials in 1996, 1997 and 2010, the Lord used the occasion to strengthen me for a new assignment. It was as if the Lord ended one major assignment and promoted me to an assignment that was even larger. Pass each test. You will need the strength it brings for the next trial.*

through the loss of two contracts, denial of my SBA certification, denial from my credit union for a mortgage modification, and more, I chose to focus on the good that was going on — the spiritual perception the Lord gave me that something was wrong in my community with young black boys being distracted. I focused on the journey the Lord was leading me on through my Leadership Maryland experience. Focusing on the good sustained me.

Each place we visited confirmed the spiritual perception I had that something was awry in my community. Each experience confirmed that I must act and do something to address the disparity I saw in incarceration. Focusing on the good that God was showing me brought me through all the trials and prepared me to past the tests. Focusing on the good sustained me so strongly that in passing the tests, it prepared me for spiritual promotion to the next higher level of purpose: my assignment, The Clarion Call. The Lord brought me through all 10 trials in 2010; all occurring simultaneously. All while the trials felt like 10 alligators were nipping at my heels. I passed all the tests and was spiritually much stronger, much more mature, and much bolder for the Lord. Focusing on the good kept my head lifted up. Now when I think of 2010, I only remember my spiritual journey and what the Lord illuminated to me through my assignment of The Clarion Call.

## THE DESIRE OF YOUR HEART

I did not realize it then, but the spiritual perception I had starting in 2008, that something was wrong in the black community, was actually the Lord preparing my heart to recognize there indeed was a problem, and He planted the seed for the desire to do something to eradicate the

> *The Lord* GIVES YOU THE DESIRE. *He plants the seed in your heart to desire to do His task, His assignment.*

problem. That seed germinated and became larger in 2009. Then the Lord provided fertile ground for that seed to sprout in my heart, through having two people recommend me to Leadership Maryland. He made it clear at the start of the LMD experience that I was not there to socialize but rather to remain in a state of perception and to discern and spiritually "see" what I was looking at. In July of 2010 at the Maryland State Prison, the Lord showed me what the problem was. He crystalized the work in my heart the day I experienced that cell door closing. At the end of the LMD experience, after the emotional and thought-provoking exchange and its impact on the class, the Lord GAVE me the desire of my heart. He planted the seed in my heart in 2008 to recognize there as a problem. Now that seed had matured from simply recognizing a problem, to the desire to take action to address the problem of mass incarceration of young black boys and men by disrupting the prison pipeline. The Lord GIVES YOU the DESIRE of your heart.

"To whom much is given, much is required" (Luke 12:48). Many strong trials will come just before you receive the illumination of your assignment. You will go through a wilderness experience, a training ground. The season of multiple strong trials is your spiritual final exam. In school, you had quizzes, tests, and the final. The final exam was always much more difficult than the tests, but you had to pass the final to be promoted to the next level. Your season of multiple simultaneous trials will be your spiritual final exam before promotion to the next level of purpose.

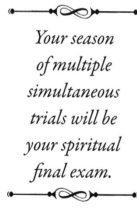

*Your season of multiple simultaneous trials will be your spiritual final exam.*

I went through the period of "ten alligators nipping at my heels" because the Lord was teaching me to completely look to Him, rely on Him, and trust Him, no matter what I was going through. Unlike Peter,

I HAD to keep my eyes on the Lord, regardless of how tumultuous the trials. I had no idea the Lord had an assignment waiting for me. I just knew keeping my eyes on the Lord was the only thing I could do to remain in a state of peace and to hold myself together.

Focusing on the good that I was experiencing in 2010, with Leadership Maryland, was an oasis of peace in the midst of the storm. The Lord knew He had the assignment of The Clarion Call waiting for me; but first I had to pass the tests — all ten simultaneous tests. God wants you to get to the point where He can trust you. You must demonstrate you can be trusted with small things before He gives you a larger task. He who is "faithful over a few things, I will make ruler over many things" (Matt. 25:21). God needs you to look to Him and rely on Him to guide you through EVERY trial. Do not look to your friends for guidance. Look to the Lord! Obey every time He leads you to do or say something. Do not go by what you "feel," or by whether you think you are capable, or by whether you think it is the right way to do it, or by whether you even understand WHY you should do it. Just obey God. Obedience brings the reward.

When you continue to pass test after test, you will mature to the place where you can embrace the trials. You will see each trial as a wink from the Lord that He is ready to promote you to the next level of purpose. But first, you must pass the test set before you. You will begin to see trials differently. Trials are an opportunity for you to be matured and spiritually strengthened by the Lord for use at a greater level. Trials are also an opportunity for the adversary to attempt to throw you off course, to distract you from what the Lord wants you to do. "Submit yourself to God, resist the devil and he will flee from you" (James 4:7). You will overcome the trial if you pour yourself into

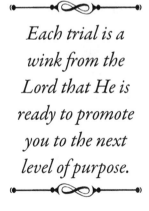

*Each trial is a wink from the Lord that He is ready to promote you to the next level of purpose.*

the Lord and have His Holy Spirit pour into you. You will go through the trial with peace of mind. "I will keep him in perfect peace whose mind is stayed on me" (Is. 26:3). Stay focused; keep your eyes on the Lord. Do not worry or focus your attention on your situation. Your situation is God's problem; He knows all about it and He knows how to best handle it. Hand your situation over to the Lord and let Jesus, who IS the Way, show you the way to resolution. You will be stronger, more mature, and better prepared for what is to come.

## TRIBULATIONS.

The Word tells us that "in the world we SHALL have tribulation, but be of good cheer, I have overcome the world" (John 16:33). God has already overcome the world, so there is nothing in the world that can keep us from doing what the Lord wants us to do. We must keep our eyes on the Lord. Do not be like Peter who took his eyes off the Lord. The moment Peter looked down and saw he was standing on the water (focused on his circumstances), he sank. Peter took his eyes off Jesus and focused his eyes on his situation, and this caused him to sink. No matter what trial or tribulation you may go through, keep your eyes on Jesus.

*God has already overcome the world, so there is nothing IN the world that can keep us from doing what the Lord wants to do.*

Remember, trials and tribulations are God's spiritual barbells to spiritually strengthen us for the assignment yet to come. The Word says we are to "Glory in tribulation; knowing that tribulation worketh patience" (Rom. 5:3). We want patience because, "In your patience possess ye your soul" (Luke 21:19). We want patience also because patience is a fruit of the Spirit. However, patience is a fruit that matures only after experiencing and overcoming trials and tribulations.

Consider every trial as a class with a test you must pass. God knows about each trial you will deal with. He knows exactly what it will take to get you through each trial. He knows just what you need to do to take care of each trial, and He will lead you step-by-step through the process. In every trial, there is a spiritual lesson you need to learn. The Lord knows the spiritual lesson you need to learn in that trial. It is your obedience in following the steps the Lord lays before you that will bring you through the trial, both naturally and spiritually. Naturally, you will be better after obediently going through the trial so that you no longer need to repeat the class. Spiritually, you will have learned the spiritual lesson the Lord wanted you to learn. You will be spiritually stronger, ready to be promoted to the next level of purpose.

## WHEN DEATH COMES

When I was in my early twenties, before my dad was to have surgery, the family prayed the surgery would go well. My dad's prayer, "Father if it is not to be so, help my family to understand that it is really with You that I would rather be. Help my family to understand that I have lived all my life just for the day when I could see Your face" – left me stunned, shocked, and perplexed. I couldn't understand how my father could say, he would rather be with dead than be with us.

At the time I was saved but I did not understand death then. I was very afraid of death. I never saw life ending. I thought, OK, so you die, and they put you in this beautiful box. Then they put you and the box in the ground. There's no light, no one to talk to; you just lay there. The box is so tight you can't even move. If a bug crawled across your nose, you couldn't even move your hand to brush it off. So, who in their right mind would ever want to die? Why would my dad want to die? I was totally perplexed.

I knew my dad loved us, and I knew my dad loved the Lord. I realized that he knew something about the Lord that I did not know. I decided right then that I wanted to know the Lord like my dad knew Him. That decision started me out on a personal quest to seek the Lord for myself.

I sought the Lord, and He heard me. I recognized His voice. I reached for Him, and He guided me. The more I followed, the more He led. The more I gave Him credit for blessings, the more He blessed. I gave Him credit for everything. Then credit turned to praise. The more I praised Him, the more of His grace, power, and joy I felt. Then I worshiped Him and found His Favor.

All of his life, well into his fifties, my father had never fallen sick. He started to lose weight rapidly and was told he had a thyroid condition. He was given radioactive iodine in the form of one pill to treat the condition. My mother was concerned the radioactive iodine would cause my father to have cancer. Doctors assured her it would not. Three months after that one pill, my father was diagnosed with cancer. The family gathered in prayer in preparation for surgery to remove the cancer on the side of his neck. After an eight-year struggle with surgery, radiation, and chemotherapy it became evident Dad was not winning the battle. His body

> *I sought the Lord, and He heard me. I recognized His voice. I reached for Him, and He guided me. The more I followed, the more He led. The more I gave Him credit for blessings, the more He blessed. I gave Him credit for everything. Then credit turned to praise. The more I praised Him, the more of His grace, power and joy I felt. Then I worshiped Him and found His favor.*

began to stiffen, causing him to be bed ridden. I asked if I could shave him. It was a badge of honor to shave my dad!

We talked of his coming departure; at least he and I talked. My mom and siblings would not talk of such a thing as death. He was not afraid. He was very peaceful. My father died in 1989. I shaved my dad in the hospital bed, after he had died.

It was because of my father that I started on a personal journey to know the Lord for myself. Today, I am grateful that I have come into a oneness with the Lord where I can say, "Father, help my family to understand that it is really with you that I would rather be. Help them to understand that I have lived all my life just for the day when I will see your face." THANK YOU, DADDY!

In February of 1996, my mother and second sister were both given a prognosis of not living beyond July that year. They were both on their death beds, and we didn't know which one was going to die first. With my sister and my mother both dying at the same time, and my baby sister pregnant for the first time, all I could focus on was being thankful that both my sister and my mother loved the Lord. I was thankful that they could find peace in all that they were going through. I was thankful that my siblings all knew the Lord, and we could find strength in each other and strength in knowing the Lord loved us all.

My baby sister died in her sleep early in the morning on Thanksgiving Day, 2016. I published the following tribute for her passing:

# "A Beautiful Passing"
### A life of a different sort...

Jewel Hatcher Bailey, aka "Cricket", passed from this life on Thanksgiving Day.
Her life, final preparations, and passing were like none I've ever heard.
Cricket is my baby sister. I share her story in hopes that it will encourage you.

---

## Gracious

Cricket delighted in life and found joy in making others happy. The ultimate organizer, she loved planning a good project. The Lord was so <u>Gracious</u> as to let Cricket know her time was near; the doctors had not told her that, but she knew. Planning her departure from this life became her new 'project'; she was exhilarated about planning every detail. She wanted to be cremated so she phoned the mortician and the crematory, ensuring they understood her plans. She wanted to ensure she would be 'comfortable' and for Cricket that meant wearing her pajamas! She bought new PJs, white laced socks and pink tennis shoes; she packed them in her 'Ever' box. She did NOT want a 'repast'. She wanted a reception with finger food and tall tables so people could meet and greet.

---

## Merciful

The Lord was <u>Merciful</u> in that Cricket was not in pain, not on life support, and not in the hospital; instead she was up and about, as effervescent as ever right until the end. Cricket and Kevin celebrated their 30th wedding anniversary dining at their favorite restaurant, just two days before she passed. She was on FaceBook with my daughter, at 10 PM the night before she passed, asking what type Legos my grandson wanted for Christmas. Cricket had many health challenges

this year; but she glorified the Lord through them all; never complaining, and always cheerful.

## Loving

God was so _Loving_ as to bring Cricket home to Himself gently and quietly, early Thanksgiving morning, while she slept. The Lord had her brother-in-law be in town for Thanksgiving, which meant her husband was not in the house alone when he found Cricket had passed.

The family carried out Cricket's wishes to be cremated; we were present for the cremation. We prayed prior to entering the furnace room. Cricket wore the PJ's, laced socks, and pink tennis shoes she had purchased for this special occasion. We took memory photos. We watched as her body was rolled into the oven, feet first. We praised the Lord for His love and kindness toward Cricket, and our family. We stayed for another hour singing praises unto the Lord for allowing us to experience such a beautiful person, life, and passing; and for experiencing HIM as a Gracious, Merciful and Loving God. It is comforting, even joyous, to experience such "A Beautiful Passing", and glorious 'welcome home.'

Cricket purchased her own urn. It is a 'living urn', meaning it is biodegradable. She wants her ashes put into her new urn and placed in the ground with a dogwood tree planted over top. She wants it planted on the grounds of our family property. We delight in doing so....

"We all know when where and how we came into this world, but none of us knows when where or how we are going to leave. We are all responsible for, and will be held accountable for what we've done with the life we've been given while here." Get ready for departure. Allow the Lord to show you how...
Blessings,
Janice

The family planted Cricket's white dogwood tree over her ashes on the family property. We held a small ceremony with a few of Cricket's sisters, her husband, son, and brother-in-law. Her husband and son planted the tree and covered it with most of the dirt. Each sister took a turn shoveling a scoop of dirt as we each said a memento to Cricket. We laughed, sang, took pictures, and captured it on video. It was her son's 21st birthday.

We are creating a garden around Cricket's tree for other siblings who want their ashes planted on the family property. I am making my departure preparations now. I, too, want to be cremated with my ashes placed in a living urn and planted in the garden on our family property. I want a pink Kwanzan cherry tree planted over my ashes on the family property at Hatcher's Haven.

*Chapter 5*

# FIGHT THE GOOD FIGHT OF FAITH

"Jesus is the author and finisher of our faith" (Heb. 12:2). Jesus has already paid the price for our salvation, for our freedom from sin, for our access to God, and for the indwelling power of His Holy Spirit in us. Jesus did it all. Now, all we must do is place our total belief and trust in Jesus, the author and finisher of our faith.

"Without Faith it is impossible to please God..." (Heb. 11:6). Since God puts such a heavy emphasis on faith, we must know and understand what faith is, why we need it, and how to exercise it.

## WHAT IS FAITH?

Faith is something that you have, not something that you do. Faith becomes a part of you; it becomes one with you and your existence. Faith is a noun; you possess it. Belief is a verb; you do it. You can exercise your faith, but you cannot do it. Believing is a mental function; you believe with your mind. Faith is a spiritual component; you become one with it. When you have faith, there is evidence that you have it in the things you do and the actions you take.

Faith is always used for God's purposes and for the benefit of others. We use our faith to please God, not to get "stuff" or please ourselves. The purpose of faith is so God could have examples in the earth to reconcile others to Christ. We need faith to be a Christ-like example. If we are to reconcile others to an invisible God, we need faith to follow as He leads. Faith enables us to follow the Lord's lead no matter what the test or trial. Faith enables us to be "steadfast and unmovable, always abounding in the work of the Lord" (I Cor. 15:58).

Faith has only to do with the unseen. "Faith is the substance of things hoped for, the evidence of things not seen" (Heb. 11:1–3). As Christ-like examples, how we conduct our lives offers hope to others as evidence of the invisible God. We become the substance of the God they cannot see. Our steadfastness, actions, conduct, attitude, kindness, and love allow others to see God through us. Faith must be seen through evidence. When the evidence is present in our lives, the unseen God becomes visible to those who don't know God and draws them to Him. Faith makes the unseen visible through our evidence and through the kindness, love, and life we live as Christ-like ones.

You cannot have faith "for" something; we can only have faith "in" God. We are not to use faith to try to get cars, houses, or anything else we can purchase. Faith is about my righteousness, not my belongings.

Three things are evident when we have faith. All three are required to follow the Lord and to carry out your assignment. They are belief, obedience, and trust (a blessed assurance which also means confidence).

- Belief comes through hearing the Word of God. We believe because we have faith in God. Because I am persuaded (have faith), I believe. Confession without faith is wishing.
- Obedience primarily addresses when the Lord instructs you to do something. Instructions are in His Word, in His Voice as He speaks to you, and in the unction of the Holy Spirit as He leads you. Obedience is required when the Lord wants something from you. Because I am persuaded, I am going to do what He says. I have confidence in the instructions of God, so I will obey without question. Faith without corresponding

action is void. "Faith without works is dead" (James 2:17, 20). Obedience builds our faith in God. **Obedience births trust**. Obedience brings the reward. "He is a rewarder of them that diligently seek Him" (Heb. 11:6b).

- Both belief and obedience are required to trust; to have confidence in God and act. Having a blessed assurance (trust) in the Lord gives that confidence. Trust enables you to act not knowing the outcome, not knowing if the action is the right action, but assured by that inner unction of the Holy Spirit as He leads. We must move forward in what He said; His way or no way.

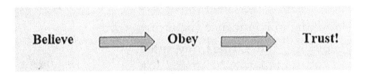

Blessed assurance (trust) will cause you to abandon anyone or anything contrary to what the Lord told you. It is what caused Noah to build the Ark when it had never rained. Belief, obedience and trust are required to exercise your faith in action and carry out the assignment the Lord has purposed for you.

Faith is not about me; it is about pleasing God. "Without faith it is impossible to please Him" (Heb. 11:6a). Many people think, "Without faith, it is impossible for God to please ME." Faith is not about getting something for yourself. It is about doing what God says to do; and usually what God says for you to do will be for the benefit of others! I get a benefit for obeying, but it is not about me benefiting. Abraham, Moses, Isaac, Jacob, and Noah all did what God said to do, for others and by faith (Heb. 11). God is not going to give you everything you want; just as a parent does not give the child everything the child wants. God wants to steer you in the way you should go. You will need faith to follow as He leads.

When I am believing, obeying, and trusting (confidence in action) I am walking (living) by faith. "The just (righteous) must live by faith" (Rom. 1:17). **Faith is about my righteousness, not my belongings.**

The purposes of faith are the following:

1) To gain access to God through faith in Jesus. You receive faith at the time of your salvation. You become the substance of your faith the moment Jesus becomes your Lord. Faith is in your spirit. Your faith and your spirit man become one. The real you, your spirit man, becomes connected with the Father. When I am walking in confidence (believing, obeying, and acting), my spirit, mind, and body are walking with God. The trinity of my person is aligned with God.

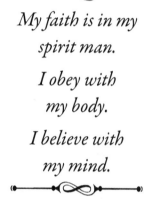

*My faith is in my spirit man.*

*I obey with my body.*

*I believe with my mind.*

2) To cause us to be yielded vessels of God. Without faith, it is impossible to please God. Faith gives you the ability to do God's work. Faith strengthens you to go against your own flesh, your carnal nature, to bring your will under subjection to the Will and Word of God.

3) To establish God's Will on the earth. If God's Will is done on the earth, all will be well. We simply need to have faith to do His Will.

## FAITH WITHOUT WORKS IS DEAD

The Scripture says, "Faith without works is dead" (James 2:20). That means, if you ask the Lord for something or ask Him to do something, YOU must also act and do something. The "doing" is your works; the doing is your faith in action. If you simply say you are "believing for" something, but you are not "doing" anything toward receiving that something, your faith is dead. Do not wait until "all your ducks are in a row" before you act. You must "walk by faith and not by sight" (2 Cor. 5:7). "The steps of a righteousness man are ordered by the Lord" (Ps. 37:23). When you ask for something with a pure heart, as you begin to take steps toward doing your part, the Lord will order (guide) your steps. The Holy Spirit is your helper. He will help you do your part if you ask for His help. He will help you do your works toward receiving what you asked.

"What **things** soever ye desire, when you pray, believe that ye receive them, and ye shall have them" (Mark 11:24).

Remember, we ask the Lord for spiritual "things" such as guidance, direction, wisdom, or protection. Do not ask God for "stuff" you can purchase. God is not an ATM machine you go to when you want new "stuff." Jesus did not suffer crucifixion so that you can have fancy "stuff." Likewise, when you ask the Lord to do something, the request should also be spiritual, such as asking Him to show you what to do in a situation, to show you how to do something you have not done before, or to lead you in handling a project or a person. Requests to the Lord for something, or to do something, must always be of spiritual focus. "God is Spirit, and those who worship Him, must worship in Spirit and in Truth" (John 4:24).

*Requests to the Lord for something, or to do something, must always be of spiritual focus.*

The Lord delights in answering us and guiding us. "In all thy ways acknowledge Him, and He will direct your paths" (Prov. 3:6). When Scripture says in "all thy ways" acknowledge Him, it means

ALL your ways! Not just the major issues or challenges, but in everything you do, need or want; take every decision, plan, or task before the Lord. "Acknowledge Him" just means ask Him. Ask the Lord to show you what to do and how to do everything, all day, every day. An example follows.

## THE SPREADSHEET

My company was pursuing a government contract, and I needed to write our proposed solution, along with the budget required to implement that solution. I had completed the proposal narrative, detailing the great solution we would bring to the agency, and exactly how we would manage the work. However, I had one day left and had not yet completed the budget for the project. At the time, my accountant was away, so I had to develop the budget myself. The contract we were pursuing would require staffing multiple employees over five years. With my accountant away, I had to use Microsoft Excel to create the spreadsheet. I had only a very basic understanding of Excel. Yet, I had to factor in labor rates, weekly hours, benefits, materials, profit, and the like. And it had to cover five years, with allowances for annual increases. I had no clue how to prepare such a thing.

I prayed and asked the Lord to prepare the spreadsheet for me. I knew I was way out of my league on this spreadsheet, but the budget was required with the proposal, and it needed to be submitted the next day. It was five o'clock in the evening when I started the spreadsheet. I prayed and started keying into the spreadsheet the position titles I proposed to staff for the project. I keyed in the number of hours each staffer would work. I asked the Lord to show me what to do. Hours later, I was still working. I took a break to refresh myself. As I headed back to the computer, I asked the Lord to please prepare this spreadsheet and to show me what to do. I sat down and started clicking something into the spreadsheet. A few hours later, I refreshed myself again, trying to stay awake. Heading back to the computer, I pleaded with the Lord to show me what to do. "Please create the spreadsheet for me." I sat down and started keying something into the spreadsheet. I was trying to think of all the items to add in. A few hours later, I refreshed myself again; it was now the middle of the night.

This went on all night long. At eight o'clock in the morning, I refreshed myself and headed back to the computer. Again, I pleaded with the Lord to create the spreadsheet for me, to show me what to do. I sat down and looked at the screen. My eyes popped wide open! I could not believe what I was seeing! The spreadsheet was fantastic! There were formulas that tabulated percentages. And when I made a change in one cell, I could see the ripple effect of the change updating all associated cells. I was astounded! There was no way I, alone, had created that spreadsheet. I flopped back in my chair in amazement and praised the Lord.

I had worked all night on that spreadsheet. I had no idea what to do or how to do it. But I prayed all night asking the Lord to please do the spreadsheet for me. The Lord never spoke to me. As I was asking the Lord to show me what to do, I was also putting my hands on the keyboard and clicking one key after the other. During the night, I had no idea what I was doing. I heard nothing from the Lord. I just kept clicking keys and praying. I did not "see" what I was creating. I did not know how to create it. But I was doing my part. I was praying AND clicking keys. I did not realize it at the time, but the Holy Spirit had guided my every click on the keyboard. If I had just prayed and sat with my hands in my lap, how would the Lord have gotten the information into the computer? If I had just prayed, how would the Lord have clicked the keys? I did the work; I clicked the keys even though I had no idea at the time what I was doing. The Lord heard my heart and He answered me; He worked through me by His Holy Spirit to prepare that spreadsheet. The Holy Spirit was guiding me with every click, in every cell. I did not realize He was working through me while

I was praying and clicking. However, it sure paid off with a spectacular spreadsheet in the end. Faith without works is dead.

## TODAY IS THE ONLY DAY FAITH WILL WORK

When you are seeking something from the Lord — a question, guidance, wisdom, understanding — His answer requires immediate action. Obey today! It is fraudulent to say you have faith when you routinely delay and put off doing what you know you are to do. When the Lord leads you to do something, He has a plan, timing, and a purpose for your task. He is also simultaneously working with other people, moving on their hearts to do something. He may be preparing that person to provide the answer to your question or to supply your needs. Your delay in acting on what the Lord leads you to do could also delay the answer to your need.

When I sought the Lord for guidance in what to do about getting another car the Lord was prompting someone else to sell their car. As I was praying and pondering with the Lord for a couple of months, the Lord was also moving on the heart of the owner of a car to put it up for sale. The Lord orchestrated the entire process of my getting that beautiful nearly new Mercedes Benz with only 23,000 miles, for only $19,000. The Lord was leading the seller and me at the same time to be in the same place for the same purpose. Had I not obeyed going from mall to mall for Milo to pee, I would not have ended up where the flashing car was — my new car.

Obey today! Today is the day to obey. Today is the day your faith will work. Your faith and obedience today prepare you for what is to come six days, six months, or six years from now. There is no need, challenge or problem in your life that Jesus does not already know about. He is already in your tomorrows, working things out on your behalf. The Lord knows what you will need, what you need to do, and who you will need to work with. He is orchestrating today, leading you today, to prepare you for what you will need next month and next year. Obeying today places you in position to receive your tomorrow blessings. Following the motto "Obey Today" is critical to being in the right place at the right time, six weeks or six months from now, to receive what God has for you. Obeying today puts your faith into action. Obeying today takes care of the works you are to do and places you in position to receive your tomorrow blessings.

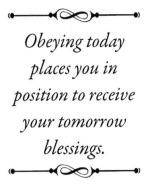

*Obeying today places you in position to receive your tomorrow blessings.*

## EMBRACE THE TRIALS

"In the world you shall have tribulation" (John 16:33). This Scripture is stated so emphatically that it sounds like a promise, and indeed, it is a fact. "In the world you SHALL have tribulation." No one makes it through life without some type of test, trial, and tribulation. But there is hope; that same Scripture goes on to say, "But be of good cheer, I have overcome the world."

God wants you to know that since tests will come, since trials will come, and since tribulations will come, be spiritually prepared. Be of good cheer because these experiences, as difficult as they may seem at the time, will be used by God as tools to teach you, strengthen you, and guide you into whom He created you to be and to do what He destined for you to do.

When we look at our current public-school system, we expect teachers to teach, strengthen, and guide students to be their best. However, students are often promoted to the next grade level even though their grade point average is exceedingly low and even though they have missed dozens of days from school with unexcused absences. Students have carried a .05 or 1.0 GPA with multiple absences and still were promoted to the next higher grade. This practice, known as "social promotion," simply passes a student along to become the next teacher's challenge to handle. These students walk across the stage with cap and gown at graduation, not realizing the emptiness of their celebration. Social promotion is a disservice to the student and society, yet it is rampant throughout many public school systems. The challenge for the student, and eventually for society, is that when that student "graduates," he will not be prepared for college, work, or life. In many instances, social promotion is a set-up for failure, often leading to the prison system. [This is a challenge addressed in my Calling.]

Using the public-school system as an analogy for spiritual growth is appropriate here for two reasons. First, both the school system and spiritual growth have many categories and levels of learning and maturity. For example, the category of elementary school has six levels, or grades, of maturity, etc. Second, they both have levels of promotion based on passing the tests (except for social promotion).

The stark exception to this parallel is that **God is not a God of social promotion!** If you do not pass the test, you **will** repeat the class.

Have you ever found yourself going through the same kind of situation time after time? Have you wondered why this situation keeps happening to you? It is because when you went through the situation the first time, there was a lesson the Lord wanted you to learn. You did not learn the lesson the first time; you failed the test, so you had to repeat the course. Hence the second situation. It may have involved different people and places, but you experienced the same type of situation. Again, there is a lesson the Lord wants you to learn through this situation; you do not learn the lesson, you fail the test. The situation repeats itself. Moreover, the same type of situation will continue to repeat itself for years to come until you learn the lesson the Lord wants you to learn. You must learn the lesson to pass the test and make the grade. You must pass the test before you can be promoted to the next higher level of spiritual maturity.

## When I Failed the Test

Over several years, the Lord orchestrated for me to take three families into my home: Felicia, Mandy, and Diane. The three family-stays occurred with a year or two between, and each stay ranged from 6 to 18 months. In each instance, I knew it was the Lord's orchestration, and they knew it as well. Felicia was a mother with one child, Diane was a mother with three children, Mandy was alone. They were each in a nearly homeless situation upon our first meeting. Each said they felt safe in my home; they thanked the Lord for being here.

I wanted each experience to glorify the Lord. I wanted them to feel at home and comfortable. I wanted them to know that while they were in my home, this is their home. In each situation, I remained humble and godly, no matter what they said or did. I wanted to be a credible witness and a godly example.

Yet, each of the three guests in my home took advantage of a safe, comfortable place to live. In each case, the guest took my kindness for weakness. Each walked over me in my own home:

- Felicia repeatedly invited personal guests with no notice to me. Moreover, she got irritated when I asked that she simply let me know in advance that she was expecting company. After my third request for notification, Felicia said, "Well, I just won't invite anyone at all. I'm not used to telling anyone that I'm going to have company." I asked Felicia to think about what she had just said — that she did not like telling anyone she was going to have company. I reminded her that each time someone had come to see me, I told her in advance that they were coming, even when my own children visited.
- Mandy, as a clothing entrepreneur, wanted to do business. I helped her start a custom design sewing business. I got lots of clients for her, transported her to client fittings, and took her

shopping for fabric. After the business was booming, I asked Mandy for $200 per month for living expenses that included the use of the whole house, utilities, internet, cable TV, and food, along with my continued business support. She got angry. Mandy had paid $60 a month for rent in the slums of Cameroon, so she thought I was ripping her off.

- Diane's car died, so she started renting cars. At the same time, she stopped contributing towards living expenses for her family of four, while she also stopped speaking to me. In Diane's instance, I had to evict. She packed all her things, took her two girls, and departed with no thank you, no key return, no goodbye. Further, she left her son! She left her son! Diane packed her belongings, drove away and left her son in my home! Diane did not care for this son. He had just turned 18, so she was no longer legally responsible. Diane's son stayed with my son and me another year.

Even though I was trying to be humble and godly, I was the common denominator in three failed tasks. Each encounter started a beautiful orchestration of the Lord, yet each experience ended ugly. I was hurt to the core because I knew God had sent each person. God did not have to chastise me because I was already hurt to my heart that I had disappointed God. Felicia, Mandy, and Diane did not know one another, so they could not have talked. I was the common denominator in each situation. I had failed the test three times. In each of these three scenarios there was something I did not learn. I asked the Lord to forgive me. I asked the Lord to show me what I did to contribute to the failure of each guest's stay in my home. I asked Him to show me what I did that I should not have done; and to show me what I did not do that I should have done.

The Lord told me, "Take the Perfecting Class." This is a class at my church that teaches the spiritual gifts. My church encourages taking the Perfecting Class every few years because the class gets updated, and because you may discover you have another gift. I had taken the class twice. The first time I took the class, I learned that I had the gift of exhortation. Exhorters encourage. I love encouraging people and drawing out their potential. The second time I took the Perfecting Class, I learned I also had the gift of leadership. It was surprising to me at the time, though I had led many efforts.

The first two times I took the Perfecting Class, I did not pay attention when they taught about the gift of mercy. Why? When I first visited the church in 1993, I purchased a taped message by Founding Pastor Cherry entitled, "Business and Economics." I was intrigued that a church taught such a topic, and I loved business. The only theme I remember from that message was the pastor saying, "If you have the gift of mercy, don't even bother going into business; you'll give the store away!" I knew the Lord had put on my heart to start a business; therefore, I rationalized that I must not have the gift of mercy. It was not that I disdained mercy; it was just that God would not give me the gift of mercy if I were in business. Right? Because, Pastor said...

Rather than me rationalizing that I must not have the gift of mercy, I should have prayed about what I had heard the pastor say, and then I should have asked God for direction. The pastor's statement was indeed true. Business owners with the gift of mercy focus on service rather than the bottom line and will often serve for free. In my home, with my three guests, I had been focused on serving them and being a godly example to the guests in my home. No matter what they did or said, I was committed to being a humble and godly Christian example. That did not work.

This time, the third time taking the Perfecting Class, I was so hurt that these three family stays had turned out ugly; I was so hurt that I had disappointed God, that when I signed up for the Perfecting Class this time, I was wide open to hear any and everything the Lord wanted me to hear.

When the Perfecting Class taught the gifts this time, I was thirsty to hear and receive. I was hoping for an answer. When they taught the gift of mercy, this time I recognized that I have the gift of mercy, big time! I have mercy dripping all off me! The challenge is, if you have not learned how to work your gift, the gift will work you. I had not realized I had the gift of mercy, so mercy was working me, and I simply thought I was being godly. **It was the gift of mercy that God used to move on my heart to help Diane, Felicia, and Mandy, and to extend my home to them as a place of rest in their time of need. However, it was that same gift that caused me to fail the test with each of them as guests in my home.** In not knowing how to use my gift of mercy, my attempts to be humble and godly were interpreted as being weak. I literally failed the test for being too kind to each of them.

I asked the Lord, "What I should do? How should I function with this gift of mercy?" The Lord told me, "In each situation, ask yourself, 'Is this a situation that requires mercy?' If it is not, don't use it." How simple! What an illumination! **The gift of mercy had been working me, but now through the guidance of the Lord, I know how to work the gift!** It is important

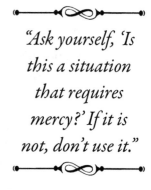

*"Ask yourself, 'Is this a situation that requires mercy?' If it is not, don't use it."*

to learn what functional gifts you have and how to work them. Every gift has a positive side and a negative side. The positive side of the gift works when you are allowing the Holy Spirit to operate the gift. The negative side manifests when the gift is operating out of your own efforts and not the leading of the Holy Spirit. In my case, I failed the test with these three guests because I did not know I had the gift of mercy, so mercy was working me! I was trying to be humble and godly at a time when I should have been firm. I was humble to people who were running over me in my own home, all the while I was thinking I was being godly no matter what they did. They were taking my kindness for weakness. I used mercy at a time when I should have been firm.

When the gifts work under Your effort, the outcome is never pleasant. Remember, everyone has at last one functional gift. Learn what your gifts are and let the Holy Spirit lead you in using them. [The functional gifts were addressed in Chapter 3.]

A year later, the Lord sent another family to stay with me under emergency circumstances; this time, it was a couple with two children. I ensured each family member felt welcomed and comfortable. However, this time when the adult did something that was not acceptable, I nipped it in the bud. I learned that you can be godly and remain firm. Lovingly, but firmly, I laid out the rules for how things would work for that type of situation. The family lived with me for six months. That was more than 10 years ago. We still have a wonderful relationship. They all call me Mama Liggins. The mother looks to me as her other mother; I see them as my family. I passed the test!

God is not a God of social promotion. We all must pass the tests put before us to move to the next level of spiritual purpose. There was a great lesson the Lord wanted me to learn: to use the gift of Mercy only in situations that require mercy. He taught me that I can be godly and loving while remaining firm.

Tests and trials will continue to come. They will come as long as we are alive on this earth. The key is to allow the Lord to lead us, teach us, and strengthen us through each test and trial so we pass the test and move to the next level of spiritual purpose.

## SPIRITUAL BARBELLS

Imagine you are sitting with your elbow on the table with a 2-pound weight in your hand, doing arm lifts. A 2-pound weight is going to give you only a tiny bit of resistance and will, therefore, produce a tiny bit of muscle strength. Then you try a 10-pound weight; there is more resistance, more effort, and more muscle strengthening. Then you try a 20-pound weight. You will have to exert a lot more energy and effort to lift that 20-pound weight because of the resistance of the weight. A heavier weight means more resistance; more effort means more muscle strength. We use weights to gain muscle strength and to make our bodies stronger.

God uses trials and tribulations as spiritual barbells! He wants to strengthen our spirit man. Just as you go to the gym, exercise, and lift weights to work out, God uses trials as spiritual weights to exercise and strengthen our spirit man. A little trial is a little weight; it requires little effort and produces little spiritual strength, but it does produce strength. The bigger the trial, the heavier the weight, the more resistance, the more effort, and the more spiritual strength gained **IF** we follow as the Lord leads to get us through the trial and to pass the test.

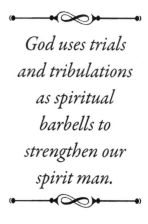

*God uses trials and tribulations as spiritual barbells to strengthen our spirit man.*

For every trial or tribulation we go through there is a lesson the Lord wants us to learn. When we do not learn the lesson, we find ourselves going through the situation again and again. God is not a god of social promotion. In God's school, the student repeats the class as many times as is necessary to learn the lesson and to pass the test. When the Lord wants you to learn a lesson, you either learn the lesson or repeat the class. To stop situations from repeating, learn the lesson God wants you to learn in each trial, each test, and each tribulation, so you pass the test the first time.

At the outset of a new trial ask the Lord:

- What is it you want me to learn?
- What do you want me to do?

- What do you want me to know?
- What am I doing that I should not do?
- What am I not doing that I should do?

You will save yourself lots of time, aggravation, and pain if at the start of a new trial, ask the Lord these questions and follow His lead.

*The purpose of the trial is to strengthen you spiritually.*

The purpose of the trial is to strengthen you spiritually. As with the example of the 2-pound, 10-pound, and 20-pound weight for arm lifts, our tests and trials will come lightweight, medium, and heavy-duty. The bigger the trial means the heavier the weight. The heavier the weight, the more resistance our spiritual muscles will encounter, and the more spiritual effort you will have to apply, and the spiritually stronger you will be in the end.

Expect your greatest trial to come from a saint — someone you know who is Christian. The reason the Christian will present your greatest trial is that it will throw you off course that the Christian behaved in a certain way. You will not expect them to conduct themselves in a carnal or ungodly manner. They are Christian, and you know they love the Lord, but their behavior, at the time, will be unlike that of a Christian. Even in the church, you will face ungodly behavior. Scripture says, "I was almost in all evil in the midst of the congregation and assembly" (Prov. 5:14). You may expect ungodly behavior from someone unsaved who does not know the Lord. It can catch you off-guard to experience persecution, malice, exclusion, ridicule, belittlement, envy, and the like from a Christian. Consider it a test for YOU; do not concern yourself with their behavior. They must pass their test, too. Pray for them. Forgive them. Love them anyway and continue to do what the Lord leads you to do.

When someone whom you know as a Christian behaves in a manner that does not glorify the Lord, you must not judge them. "Judge not, that ye be not judged. For with what judgment ye judge, ye shall be judged" (Matt. 7:1–2). We do not know why someone does what they do or behaves the way they behave. We have no way of knowing what is going on in their lives. The Lord could be working in their lives as well. We must simply pray, forgive, and love them.

- Praying for them will free you from wondering why they acted a certain way.
- Forgiving them will free you from keeping your thoughts on that person, and you will be better able to keep your focus on yourself and on what the Lord told you to do.
- Loving them will keep your heart right and ensure your behavior is that of a credible witness.

There is a lesson we must learn in every trial and tribulation. Consider each trial as a class that you must pass. The Lord wants you to learn something now that you will need to know in the future; He wants you to become spiritually stronger (mature) to handle the bigger trials that He knows will come. Tests will always start light-weight with small trials (like elementary school work). They will represent a 2-pound weight — little effort, little strengthening. Ask the Lord what it is He wants you to learn, to do, or to know. Ask Him to show you how you need to change. Ask Him to search your heart and remove anything that does not please Him. Ask Him to order your steps and guide you in the way you should go. As you ask the Lord to order your steps, remember "the steps of a **righteous** man are ordered by the Lord" (Ps. 37:23). Keep in right-standing with the Lord so He can order your steps.

Learning the lesson in the trial will enable you to pass the test and stop that scenario from repeating. Learning the lesson will spiritually strengthen you for what is to come. The tests, trials, and tribulations will continue to come; that is life. Just remember that your Heavenly Father is omniscient; the Lord already knows your present situation and your future. He is omnipresent; He is already in your tomorrows, working things out on your behalf. He knows the challenges you will face down the road. He is omnipotent; He has the power and will empower you to pass all the tests and carry out all the tasks to come. He loves you so much that He wants to strengthen you now, to prepare you to handle the tougher challenges when they come. And, they will come.

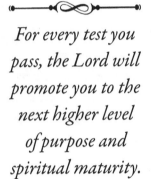

*For every test you pass, the Lord will promote you to the next higher level of purpose and spiritual maturity.*

For every test you pass, the Lord will promote you to the next level of purpose and spiritual maturity. Once you pass this test, the next trial will be bigger; just as you move to heavier weights in the gym, the next trial will be a heavier spiritual barbell. Though the next trial may be bigger, you will also be stronger and able to bear it. Apply the same process: ask the Lord to show you what it is He wants you to learn, to do, and to know. Ask the Lord to search your heart and show you where you need to change. Ask Him to order your steps.

Indeed, God is not a god of social promotion. He will not promote you to the next level of purpose until you have learned what He wants you to learn in the current trial.

## FEAR

When the Lord tells us to do something and we resist, rebel, refuse, or are reluctant, it may be fueled by fear. Perhaps it is something we have never done before. Perhaps it is bigger than what we can do alone, and we are afraid to try. Fear is not of God. Fear is another tactic of the adversary to throw us off course.

When God tells us to do something, we can EXPECT challenges to come.

When God tells us to do something, we can EXPECT people to doubt us.

When God tells us to do something, we can EXPECT the adversary to show up.

When God tells us to do something, we can ALSO EXPECT that God will see us through!

What has the Lord told you to do that you have yet to start? What has He put on your heart to do but you are still questioning whether you can do it? Who has the Lord told you to help whom you still have not contacted? You may be waiting for the Lord to answer one thing, while He's waiting for you to do the last task He told you to do. You are holding up your own progress!

God wants His children to obey. Go back through your memory bank and pull out every incomplete or untouched task the Lord gave you. Finish each one. When we question whether we can do something the Lord told us, or when we waste precious time deciding if we really heard from God, we are operating in fear.

What causes fear? Fear is caused by looking at our situation, like Peter did when he was walking on the water, rather than keeping our focus on what God said. Fear is caused by considering the FACTS rather than the TRUTH. Fear builds when we are slothful in obeying the Lord. Fear builds when we question God and are disobedient to Him. Fear is the opposite fruit of what righteousness produces.

Fear is what happens when we are not in truth. Jesus is the truth. When we are operating in the Will of God, with the indwelling power of the Holy Spirit, we are walking in truth. We know that we cannot do the work on our own, but we also know that the Lord is with us, and it is HE who will do the work.

What does fear cause? Fear paralyzes us. It paralyzes our thinking. Fear causes us to believe our situation is our reality rather than focus on the truth of what God said. Fear takes our focus from what we know to what we see, hear, and feel. Fear pulls us into the natural, into the flesh. Fear causes us to miss the mark. It steals our commitment and destroys our witness. We cannot do God's Will when we are in fear. "God has not given us a spirit of fear; but of power, and of love, and of a sound mind" (2 Tim. 1:7).

Why should we fear not? "Fear not" is used in the Bible 71 times: 55 in the Old Testament and 16 times in the New Testament. When we do not obey because of fear, we do not trust God. We trust God only as much as we obey Him. The only way to progress in your calling or assignment is through obedience to the Will and Word of God. The only way to reach fulfillment in your assignment is to obey the Word and instructions of the Lord — each time, every time. Remember, obedience brings the reward.

Fear nothing and no one. "Fear not them which kill the body, but are not able to kill the soul: but rather fear him which is able to destroy both soul and body in hell" (Matt. 10:28). Do not worry about what others may think, say, or do. Fear the Lord. When you are doing what the Lord said to do, you already have the victory.

How do we overcome fear? Focus on the truth of God's Word. God said, "I will never leave you or forsake you" (Heb. 13:5). God is Jehovah Jireh, our provider. We are "more than conquerors, through Him that loved us" (Rom. 8:37). God gave you a sound mind. What you see is less important than what you know. Pray this: "Take my eyes off what I see and put my spiritual eyes back onto what I know. I know God loves me. I know I am a child of the Most-High God. I know God will make a way for me." Focus on what the Lord has led you to do, not on your current circumstances.

When you have overcome fear, you will obey without full understanding. You will obey today. You will walk by faith and not by sight. You will keep moving, putting one foot in front of the other, even when things do not make sense to your natural mind. Your light will shine and draw others to the Lord. You will be a vessel for the Lord to use as HE chooses. You will be bold in your witness of who you are, and of *whose* you are as a child of the Most-High God.

## WRESTLE NOT AGAINST FLESH AND BLOOD

You will assuredly encounter obstacles whenever you obey the Lord. The adversary will always be attempting to distract you from doing what the Lord wants done. We have an adversary, and he does not want to see you succeed in doing the work of the Lord. God is Spirit, and the adversary is a spirit. The Lord needs willing vessels to do His work here on earth, as does the adversary.

> "For we wrestle not against flesh and blood, but against principalities, against powers, against the rulers of the darkness of this world, against spiritual wickedness in high places" (Eph. 6:12).

The Lord gives each of us free choice in whom we will obey. The Word says, "To whom you yield yourself servant to obey, his servant you are to whom you obey" (Rom. 6:16). So when you continually do things that are not of God, especially when you know they are not of God, you are choosing to obey the devil and to be his servant. However, God's desire is for each of us to choose the Lord. He tells us, "I have set before you life and death, blessing and cursing: choose life" (Deut. 30:19). God tells us to choose life. The Word also tells us that Jesus is the Life. "Jesus is the Way, the Truth, and the Life" (John 14:6). Every person has the same choice to make in whom they are going to serve.

There are only two options: Jesus or the devil. Jesus is the only Way to Heaven. "No man cometh to the Father, but by Jesus" (John 14:6).

We were all "born in sin and shaped in inequity" (Psalms 51:5). From birth, we all had a sin nature; we were born with a natural inclination to resist God. Until, and unless, we choose to give our lives to Jesus as our Savior and our Lord, we remain in our sin nature. Even after salvation, if you are not diligent in your walk with the Lord, you can find yourself operating in your sin nature, out of your carnal mind. When you focus on the natural, and on the things you want to acquire, and on having the biggest and the best, be careful. You are opening yourself to being tempted by the adversary. The adversary thrives on people who focus on the natural, who think with a carnal mind rather than a spiritual mind. He looks for people who focus on acquiring stuff more than on obeying the Lord. The adversary thrives on people who allow him to lead them. These people look like you and me. They work with you, ride the train with you, shop where you shop, and go to church with you. The adversary will use whoever allows him to entice them with worldly pleasures.

If you are not careful, the adversary will use you! If you slack off your devotion and let your "flesh" guide your decisions, and if you choose to add or alter what the Lord said to do, you'll find yourself in a desolate place. When you fight the good fight of faith, sometimes you will have to fight against yourself and your desires. No one else can stop you on your journey to your calling. Only you can stop you.

## SEE WHAT YOU ARE LOOKING AT

When your co-worker schemes against you to jockey for promotion, is that God leading them? When your neighbor runs over your child's bike and refuses to pay for it, is that God? When the person in your volunteer group takes the credit for all the work you did, is that God? When people do things that we know are not of God, do not take it personally and do not charge it to them. And don't judge them. Recognize that the adversary needs to work through someone to throw YOU off course. This will usually be someone you know. Sometimes, the scheme or attack will come from someone in the church. This doesn't mean that person is of the devil; it means for that moment, they let their spiritual guard down enough to allow the adversary room to get in. Just as God needs someone to do His work, the devil needs people to work through too. The devil presents and persuades. He will present enticing opportunities, things, and people and try to persuade you to bite. The adversary will use whomever he can — whoever accepts his temptation. The adversary will try one enticement after the other just to distract you from doing God's work. He will use whomever he can to throw you off course from doing the work of the Lord. He wants nothing more than to destroy your relationship with the Lord. Never focus on what someone else does. God will take care of them; just keep your eyes on Jesus!

"Wait on the Lord and keep His way, and He shall exalt thee to inherit the land; when the wicked are cut off, thou shall see it" (Ps. 37:34). This is another of those promises with conditions.

The promise: He shall exalt thee to inherit the land; and when the wicked are cut off, thou shall see it.

The condition: (We must first) Wait on the Lord and keep His way (*wait* here means serve the Lord).

This Scripture brings a blessed assurance. It tells us that if we continue to serve the Lord, and if we stay humbly in His Will, the Lord will fight our battle, and we will win. Then, when those who were against us are defeated, we will see their downfall.

I saw this Scripture manifest in my life when I was a young adult, even before I knew it was Scripture. There were several situations where God gave me the victory when others were acting ugly towards me.

After one significant incident, I was reading the Bible and saw this Scripture for the first time; I almost dropped my Bible. I had no idea this was in the Scriptures. It was as if God was speaking directly to me for that situation, letting me know He was with me. God had just won a battle for me; I had just seen the other person defeated. I felt sorry for them for acting so ugly, and they were now receiving God's chastisement. When I read the Bible, it blessed me to no end to see this Scripture at that moment. God, Himself, reassured me He was with me. This was comforting and strengthening at the same time. This scenario also demonstrates that the Word is true. Even if we do not know the Word, it is still true. God had demonstrated this Scripture to me several times before me ever reading it in the Bible. God's Word is true whether we believe it, realize it, or receive it.

Do not worry about the person who is treating you mean or ugly; pray for them. The person is not against you; it is the adversary. Moreover, do not concern yourself with the adversary; he is God's problem. Let the Lord handle the adversary. Stay focused on the Lord and on what the Lord told you to do. "Wait on the Lord and keep His way, and He shall exalt thee to inherit the land; when the wicked are cut off, thou shall see it" (Ps. 37:34).

Do not try to fight your battle; let the Lord fight for you. Let the Lord fight through you. Do not attempt to fix things or work it out on your own. "The weapons of our warfare are not carnal [natural], but mighty through God to the pulling down of strongholds" (2 Cor. 10:4). A stronghold is any habit, lifestyle, addiction, thinking, belief, or person that continuously hinders you from doing the Will of the Lord. Prayer is the weapon of your warfare. Prayer will pull down any stronghold that is hindering you or your work.

*Prayer is the weapon of your Warfare.*

## ASK THE LORD FOR WISDOM

Wisdom comes only from the Lord. Solomon, the wisest man ever created, asked God for wisdom. "A man's wisdom maketh his face to shine, and the boldness of his face shall be changed" (Ecc. 8:1). Wisdom is insight and understanding on how to apply knowledge to carry out the Lord's instructions expediently, for the benefit of others. Wisdom releases when our work is for the benefit of others.

"Wisdom is the principal thing; therefore get wisdom: and with all your getting, get understanding" (Prov. 4:7). God will give wisdom freely, but you must ask for it. "If any of you lack wisdom, let him ask of God, that giveth to all men liberally, and upbraideth not; and it shall be given him" (Jas. 1:5).

The longer you serve the Lord, obey Him, and trust Him, and the more you go through trials and tests with Him, the more wisdom you will acquire in the process. Wisdom is essential in doing the Will of the Lord for others. Your calling, whatever it may be, will involve you doing something for others. You will need wisdom to carry out your assignment. Wisdom enables you to see past a person's behavior, to see their hurt, and to genuinely have a heart to help. Wisdom knows how to help the person in a manner that is beneficial to them spiritually and naturally. Wisdom loves unconditionally. "But the wisdom that is from above is first pure, then peaceable, gentle, and easily entreated, full of mercy and good fruits, without partiality, and without hypocrisy" (Jas. 3:17).

## FORGIVENESS

Forgiveness is a huge thing to God! *Forgive* is referenced 95 times in the Bible. *Forgiveness* is referenced 8 times. Mark 11:25 says, "And when you stand praying, forgive, if you have ought against any: that your Father also which is in Heaven may forgive you your trespasses."

This is another example of a promise that has a condition, except this promise requires you to give your permission (through your action) before the Lord will act:

Promise: Your Father also **may** forgive you your trespasses.
Condition: When you stand praying, forgive.

If we pray with unforgiveness in our hearts, can the Lord even receive our prayer? If we have unforgiveness against others, the Lord has yet to forgive us of our transgression. Your unforgiveness towards others hinders your own prayers from being answered by the Lord.

In 2 Corinthians 2:10, Paul tells us, "To whom ye forgive anything, I forgive also..." When you forgive, always forgive in the name of Jesus. Forgive even if the perpetrator hurt your friend and not you directly. If your hurt friend forgives them, then you should also forgive them in the name of Jesus. "Lest Satan should get an advantage of us: for we are not ignorant of his devices" (2 Cor. 2:11). Indeed, the adversary has many devices. One of the devil's devices is our unforgiveness. As Christians, we have a significant role in helping others be in right standing with God. If we forgive a person for something, God will also forgive that person for that something. "To whom ye forgive anything, I forgive also:" (2 Cor. 2:10)

How awesome is our God! How merciful is He to extend to us the grace of forgiveness to others!

Perhaps a loved one or a family member did something that hurt you deeply. Perhaps what they did caused you great financial loss. Perhaps it was emotionally draining. Perhaps it was not what they did, but rather what they did not do. Perhaps you feel you could hate them and feel justified in your right to hate them. Not so. Regardless of the emotional pain or the financial loss, you must forgive them. It must be from your heart, in the name of Jesus, kind of forgiveness.

People are going to hurt you. Hurt comes with life. Some of those people may be people you love who are closest to you. But do not worry; God sees all, He knows all, and He cares. The Lord will hold that person accountable for what they did, just as He will hold you accountable for how you handle yourself in response to what they did.

The best way to get beyond the pain and hurt that someone caused you is for you to pray for them. Pray fervently for them. You may need to pray so fervently for them that you cry, snot and snort. You may need to lay prostrate on the floor, stand, sit, and pace around the room as you pray. You might yell to the top of your lungs as you pray for the other person. You may pray for an hour, just for the Lord to bless that person. In the end, YOU will be blessed!

I have prayed for someone like this. Yes, I have cried, snotted and snorted while pacing, lying prostrate on the floor, or yelling at the top of my lungs. At the end of my hour-long prayer, I was showered with overflowing peace and calm deep in my soul; it was beautiful! I felt like I had just stood under Niagara Falls, and all the frustration I once felt had gotten thoroughly washed away! It was such a peaceful, surreal experience, that I thought, "Oh, Father! Who else is messing with me?" I wanted to pray for everybody! It was an amazing feeling.

Rather than being bitter and angry at those who hurt us, as Christians, we are to love our enemies. "Bless them that curse you, do good to them that hate you, and pray for them which despitefully use you, and persecute you" (Matt. 5:44). As Christ-like ones, we must pray for those very people who hurt us; pray for them and forgive them.

No matter what a person has done to you or to someone you love, forgive them. No matter what a person has neglected to do, forgive them. Forgiveness is ultimately for your sake. Harboring the hurt or wrong someone did to you will only cause you to have a bitter heart; **God cannot use a bitter heart.** If you want to be in right standing with the Lord, you must forgive. We must maintain a forgiving spirit. If you want the Lord to forgive YOU of your trespasses, you must forgive others first! "But, if you do not forgive, neither will your Father in Heaven forgive your trespasses" (Mark 11:26). You cannot please the Lord with a bitter heart.

Unforgiveness is like a cancer destroying the foundation of any progress you try to make with the Lord. We have all been through challenges where someone hurt us in one way or another. I could write a book about deeds others have done or not done; I won't but I could.

*"I need Jesus more than I need anybody breathing!"*

None of the people or the challenges they take us through is worth our relationship with the Lord. You must make up your mind that no one is worth your relationship with the Lord. My motto is, **"I need Jesus more than I need anybody breathing!"** This is true for all of us. We all need Jesus! We all depend on Him every day for everything. We may get so busy in the hustle and bustle of life that we sometimes forget that major point. Never waste your time stewing over someone, or what someone did, or did not do. Rather, focus on how the Lord brought you through it all. You are still here. You are still moving forward. You deserve better than to let yourself wallow in past hurts or past mistakes. Forgive them. It is freeing for **you**! Forgive yourself. It is even more freeing!

## SPIRITUAL WARFARE

We are at war and in a spiritual warfare. We are at war because we have an adversary, the devil. Every day you wake up, sit up in your bed, and swing your feet down to the floor, you are stepping onto the battlefield. Every day, the adversary is going to be on his job. "The devil comes to steal, kill, and destroy" (John 10:10). He seeks to kill relationships, steal opportunities, and destroy your potential. Every day, he is going to try to wreak havoc in whatever situation you allow him to enter. Daily, the adversary "walketh about seeking whom he may devour" (1 Pet. 5:8). He seeks whomever he can distract from doing the work of the Lord. He seeks to destroy your plans to accomplish the task or assignment the Lord has instructed you to do.

It is not your job to fight the devil. You will lose every time. Your job is to "Submit yourselves therefore to God. Resist the devil, and he will flee from you" (James 4:7). Resisting the devil strengthens you to no longer be tempted by things he presents to you, or things he tries to persuade you to do. Resisting the devil while submitting yourself to God strengthens you against fleshly temptation as you do the work of the Lord.

That does not mean the devil will not attack; he is the devil, and attack is what he does. The devil knows he may no longer be able to tempt you, but he will certainly continue to attack just to see if your guard is down. Resisting the devil while submitting yourself to God strengthens you to be a soldier for the Lord.

## SOLDIERS IN THE ARMY OF THE LORD

Soldiers fight the good fight of faith (1 Tim. 6:12). The good fight of faith is obeying the instructions of the Lord, knowing that Jesus has already won the war. Fighting the good fight of faith is moving forward in what the Lord has told you to do, no matter what obstacles or hindrances may appear to be in your way. If the Lord told you to do something, the devil is going to try to stop you by distracting you and causing you to doubt. Pray your way through! Ask the Lord what to do, how to do it, when, where, and with whom to do the work. He will lead you through or around anything that may stand in your way.

As soldiers in the Army of the Lord, to be successful in battle, we must use the proper battle gear. We must daily prepare for battle by shoring up our armor, the whole armor of God. We must fight the good fight of faith, realizing that "the weapons of our warfare are not carnal, but are mighty through God to the pulling down of strongholds" (2 Cor. 10:4).

We have a Helper in the Holy Spirit. The Holy Spirit will help you to fight the battle. He will help you do whatever the Lord told you. Note, however, that the Holy Spirit is our Helper; He will help do the work through you, but He will not do the work for you.

We can do nothing the Lord asks of us on our own. That is because "the battle is not yours, but God's" (2 Chron. 20:15). "The Lord strong and mighty; the Lord mighty in battle" (Ps. 24:8). It is He, in you, "who doeth the work" (John 14:10). The Lord wants to do the work through you. He does not expect you to do the work on your own. Any task the Lord gives you to do will be larger than what you can do on your own anyway, so do not even think to do it on your own. God wants you to obey and trust Him as He leads you in each task. He wants to empower you with the indwelling power of His Holy Spirit. With the power of the Holy Spirit in you, you "can do all things through Christ Jesus who strengthens you" (Phil. 4:13). "Be strong in the Lord and in the power of His might" (Eph. 6:10).

The Old Testament in the Bible uses terms like *soldiers, fight, wrestle, battle, warfare, armor, enemy,* and *adversary* for a reason. We are at war. We are at war with the adversary. The New Testament uses terms like *obey, trust,* and *faith.* That is because Jesus sacrificed His life to win the war over sin and death. Jesus has already won the war, and we can be successful in the battle IF we obey, trust, and walk in faith.

In military battle, the general, the commanding officer, gives the orders on who, how, and when to fight. The soldier follows orders and fights no matter how heavy the battle is raging. The soldier stays in position and fights, even unto death.

We are soldiers in the army of the Lord. We are His hands, His legs, and His voice. We are His soldiers, together His troop, to fight the battle. "The battle is not yours, but God's" (2 Chron. 20:15). God will put you in jobs, churches, neighborhoods, programs, and families for HIS purposes. Just like the general, God, your commanding officer, will give you orders or instructions. When things start going opposite to what you want, or slower than you want, or if they get tougher than you expected, you cannot quit and run.

How can the commanding officer ever win a battle if the soldiers decide they don't like the way the battle is going, so they pick up their weapons and march off the battlefield? Do soldiers pout and whine to the commanding officer, saying, "I don't want to play anymore"? No! No war is won with quitters.

We are soldiers in the army of the Lord. We are in spiritual warfare, and we must stay in position. If the Lord sent you there, He needs you there. If He sent you to a church, job, or program, there is something He needs you to do there. We must stay in position no matter how tough the battle rages. We stay and let the Lord fight the battle for us and through us. We know that "the weapons of our warfare are not carnal but mighty through God to the pulling down of strongholds" (2 Cor. 10:4). We must "fight the good fight of faith" (1 Tim. 6:12), knowing that the battle is not ours, but it is the Lord's. We stay in position and fight with prayer, obedience, faith, and trust. The Lord has need of you there. He has plans for you there. Your reward of obedience is there.

Don't ask friends what you should do. Ask the Lord, and follow as He leads, whatever that may be — all the time, every time. Wherever the Lord sends you, stay until He sends you somewhere else.

## THE WHOLE ARMOR OF GOD

In 2004, I was reading Scripture in Ephesians 6:11 about the whole armor of God. The Lord showed me the significance of the armor of God and why every believer must shore up his armor daily. The Lord inspired me to use the Scripture in Ephesians to create a prayer. I call the prayer "Shoring Up Your Armor: Daily Preparation for Spiritual Warfare."

The prayer has a purpose, goal, and objective, along with the rationale for why the armor is critical for every believer.

**Purpose:** To create a visible and tangible impression of the armor of God in the mind of the believer.

**Goal:** To cause the believer to see the importance of using, and the danger of not using, the armor daily.

**Objective:** To cause the believer to prepare himself for spiritual warfare daily by shoring up his armor.

**Rationale:** Every morning as we awaken, sit on the bed and swing our feet down to the floor, we are stepping onto the battlefield. Every day the adversary is certain to do his part in attempting to throw us off the straight and narrow path. Every day he will attempt to distract you from doing whatever the Lord wants you to do that day.

As Christians, we live in two worlds: spiritual and natural. We cannot focus only on natural preparation and ignore spiritual preparation. If we simply get up and out in the natural each morning, we are leaving ourselves vulnerable to the attacks of the enemy, and the enemy will attack. Every day, he will attack. Every day, we will be vulnerable. If we get up and start our day without our armor, it is equivalent to a military soldier going to Iraq or Afghanistan with nothing on but his skivvies. He, assuredly, will get hurt. Military soldiers prepare for battle. They put on battle gear: helmets, bulletproof vests, and boots. And they most definitely pick up their weapons.

As soldiers in the army of the Lord and warriors on the battlefield, we too must be equipped. Scripture tells us to "put on the whole armor of God that we are able to stand against the wiles of the devil. For we wrestle not against flesh and blood, but against principalities, against powers, against the rulers of the darkness of this world, against spiritual wickedness in high places" (Eph. 6:11–12).

Spiritual warfare requires spiritual battle gear. Prepare daily for battle before stepping onto the battlefield upon getting out of bed. Daily, Shore Up Your Armor.

## Shoring Up Your Armor
*Daily Preparation for Spiritual Warfare*

| | Scripture |
|---|---|
| Dear Heavenly Father, in the name of Jesus, thank you for calling me to be a soldier in your Army, a warrior on the battlefield. Thank you that the battle is not mine, Lord, but it is yours; it is you who doeth the work. Thank you that I fight the good fight of faith. Thank you that the weapons of my warfare are not carnal but are mighty through God for the pulling down of strongholds. Thank you that I am strong in you, Lord, and in the power of Your might. | 2 Chron. 20:15<br><br>1 Tim. 6:12<br>2 Cor. 10:4<br><br><br><br>Eph. 6:10 |
| **Thank you that I take on the whole armor of God, that I stand against the wiles of the devil. Thank you that after having done all, I still stand!** | Eph. 6:11<br><br>Eph. 6:13 |
| **Thank you that I stand, having my loins girded about with truth.** | Eph. 6:14 |
|     Jesus is the truth. He is the way, the truth, and the life. | John 14:6 |
|     Thank you that because Jesus girds me about with truth, I am not beguiled. | Eph. 6:14 |
|     Thank you that I see truth, know truth, live truth, believe truth, receive truth, perceive truth, and proclaim truth. | |
|     Bless Lord, that I may speak truth and bring truth into every situation and every conversation, to your glory, and to your honor. | |

Thank you that truth reigns in my heart, my mind, my home, my sphere of influence. Thank you that truth reigns.

**Thank you that I stand wearing the breastplate of righteousness.** — Eph. 6:14

It is only through righteousness that I can please you, or serve you, or be a credible witness for you. — Isa. 42:6

It is only through righteousness that I can even receive the things I need, for your Word says to seek ye first the Kingdom of God and your righteousness and you would add unto me the things such as I have need. — Matt. 6:33

Thank you that all of my needs are met according to your riches in glory by Christ Jesus. — Phil. 4:19

Thank you that you are Jehovah Jireh, You are my provider. — Gen. 22:12-14

It is only through righteousness that you will order my steps. For Your Word says the steps of a righteous man are ordered by the Lord. I pray you find me right in your sight, Father. Search my heart, Lord, and remove anything that does not please you. Give me a pure heart. — Psa. 37:23

Search my mind, Father, and remove any thought that does not please you. Give me the mind of Christ. — 1 Cor. 2:16

Order my steps, Lord. Guide me in the way you would have me to go. Guide my mind, my thoughts, my words, my actions, my reactions, my perceptions, my demeanor, my attitude, my emotions, my disposition, my countenance, and my body language, such that all that I say, and all that I do, will bless and glorify your holy name.

| | |
|---|---|
| Thank you that because I confess my sins, you are faithful and just to forgive me and to cleanse me from all unrighteousness. | 1 Jn. 1:9 |
| Thank You that You are Jehovah Tsidkenu, the Lord my righteousness. | Jer. 23:6 |

**Thank you that I stand with my feet shod with the preparation of the Gospel of Peace.** — Eph. 6:15

| | |
|---|---|
| Thank you that you keep my mind in perfect peace because it is stayed on you. | Isa. 26:3 |
| Thank you for peace that passeth understanding. | Phil. 4:7 |

Bless that I speak peace, and bring peace into every situation and every conversation, to your glory, and to your honor.

Thank you that peace reigns in my heart, my home, my life, my assignment, and my sphere of influence. Thank you that peace reigns.

| | |
|---|---|
| Thank you that You are Jehovah Shalom, my peace. | Judges 6:24 |
| Thank you that Jesus is my Prince of Peace. | Isa. 9:6 |

**Thank you that above all, I stand taking the shield of faith, wherewith I quench all the fiery darts of the wicked.**

Eph. 6:16

Thank you for the shield of faith.

It is only through faith that I can obey you without full understanding.

It is only through faith that I can do the things you tell me to do, even when they don't make sense to my natural mind.

It is only through faith that I can carry out my assignment and finish my course.

Thank you for the spiritual gifts you imparted unto me, even those that I am not aware of as of yet. I decrease that you increase in me, Father. Bless that each gift works by faith in accordance with your will and your way.

Rom. 12:6-8

Thank you that I fight the good fight of faith.

1 Tim. 6:12

Thank you that no weapon formed against me shall prosper.

Isai. 54:17

Thank you that you bless whatsoever I set my hands to do, to prosper.

Thank you that you are my *Rereward*. You've got my back!

Joshua 6:13

Thank you for the angels you've encamped round about me.

Angels, I dispatch you in the name of Jesus! Go before me and make the way plain and the path clear.

**Thank you, Lord that I stand taking on the helmet of salvation.** Eph. 6:17

> Thank you for Jesus. Thank you for saving my soul.
> Thank you for calling me to be your child. Thank
> you for growing me up into you. Thank you for Eph. 4:15
> maturing me. Thank you for purging, pruning, and
> perfecting me.
> It is only through salvation that I can call you
> Abba, Daddy. Mark 14:36
> It is only through salvation that I can call you Ishi, Hosea 2:16
> my husband.
> It is only through salvation that I have access to Eph. 2:18
> you and insight into the supernatural things of that
> place called unity.
> Thank you for reconciling me back to you. 1 Cor. 7:11
> Thank you for Jesus, the savior of my soul.
> Thank you Jesus, for keeping your promise to send Eph. 1:13
> your blessed Holy Spirit.
> Holy Spirit, I yield myself to You.
> Have Your Will and have it your way.
> Thy Will be done in me, with me, by me, for me, to
> me, and through me, in Jesus' name.

**Thank you that I stand taking the sword of the spirit, which is Your Word.**　　Eph. 6:17

    Bless that I speak your Word and bring your Word
    into every situation and every conversation.

    Thank you that your Word does not return void, but　　Isa. 55:11
    it accomplishes the thing it is set out to do.

    Thank you that your Word is medicine to my flesh　　Prov. 3:8
    and marrow to my bones.

    Thank you that you are the God who heals me.　　1 Pet. 2:24

    Thank You that by your stripes, Lord Jesus, I
    am healed.

    Thank you that I know you as Jehovah Rophe,　　Exo. 15:22-26
    my healer.


**Lord God, thank you that I pray always with all prayer and supplication in the Spirit for the saints.**　　Eph. 6:18

    Holy Spirit I offer my voice to You.

    Let Your Anointing fall fresh on me.

    Pray those things for me, and through me, that I　　Rom. 8:26
    know not what I ought to pray.

    Thank you, Father, for your Holy Spirit.

    Thank you that utterance is given to me; that I open　　Eph. 6:19
    my mouth boldly, to make known the hidden mys-
    tery of the Gospel.

    Heavenly Father, give me the interpretation of that
    which the Holy Spirit prays, that it may be profit-
    able to my natural mind.

{Pray in the Spirit}

Thank you, Father, for hearing my prayer!
Thank you that you answer my prayer!                    Eph. 5:13
Thank you, Father, that after having done all, I
STILL STAND!

In Jesus' name I pray.
In Jesus' name I trust.
In Jesus' name, I give you thanks.
AMEN

Use the armor prayer during your daily morning devotion. Shore up your armor every day! Of course, please feel free to modify this prayer to suit your own relationship with the Lord, your personality, your schedule, etc. You may not be able to pray the entire prayer every day, and if you can't, you can't. However, no matter how hurried your schedule is, you need to shore up your Armor, daily. At least, thank God that you take on the whole armor of God. Remember, it is to protect YOU against the wiles of the devil.

When I pray this prayer, I stand as firm as a soldier. I speak loudly and boldly. I envision each piece being placed upon my body as I pray the armor prayer.

Pray in the Spirit every day! You are spirit living in a natural world, and you have an adversary, the devil. Things are going on around you every day that you may not be aware of. There could be a pending accident. There may be a decision coming on your job that could negatively affect you. There could be a person you think is a friend but who is a distraction to your walk. You may not know about these things, but the Holy Spirit — God in you — knows.

Praying in the Spirit is giving God permission to pray through you, about those matters you do not know need prayer (Romans 8:26).

*Chapter 6*

# LOVE, THE GREATEST COMMANDMENT

L ove is the principal thing. Throughout the Bible, in both the Old Testament and New Testament, LOVE is referenced 442 times. God places a strong emphasis on love because **God IS Love** (1 John 4:8). God loved us enough to give His only begotten Son to save us from sin. Moreover, His Son, our Lord and Savior Jesus Christ, loved us enough to sacrifice His life for us.

## LOVE GOD.

Loving God must be your priority — the preeminent act in your mind, heart, and soul with every fiber of your being. The Word tells us, "Thou shalt love the Lord thy God with all thy heart, and with all thy soul, and with all thy mind, and with all thy strength: this is the first commandment" (Mark 12:30). The very fiber of your being must manifest your love of God. All that you say, all that you do, how you act, and how you react should demonstrate your sincere love and commitment to the Lord.

"We love Him, because He first loved us" (1 John 4:19). Like a mother with her newborn baby, the mother loves the baby even though the baby has no concept of what love is. The mother loves the baby even though the baby is totally self-centered and focused only on his own needs. The mother loves the baby even as it grows and begins to rebel. God loved us when we had no concept of what love was. He loved us even when we totally focused on our own needs. And, He loves us even when we rebel against His Will for us.

Our love of God, and our love for God, must motivate everything we do. If love is not our motivation, then selfishness will motivate us; we will love hoping to receive the things we want. God knows our hearts. God knows our thoughts before we think them; He knows our actions before we do them; He knows whether we love Him sincerely or not. Love God for who He is; the One who created you, comforts you, and sustains your life.

Love God for all that He has already done for you, not for what you want Him to do for you. God knows what you need. "God will supply all your needs according to His riches in glory by Christ Jesus" (Phil. 4:19). God knows every individual thing we need, but He wants us to first, seek Him. "But seek ye first the kingdom of God, and His righteousness; and all these things shall be added unto you" (Matt. 6:33).

We do not demonstrate our love for God simply by going to church on Sunday morning. That is the least we should do, out of obedience, "not forsaking the assembling of ourselves together" (Heb. 10:25). Nor do we demonstrate love when we thank God because everything is going our way. Neither do we demonstrate love when we **forget** to worship God because everything is going our way. Love is consistent. We demonstrate our sincere love for the Lord in good times and in difficult times. It is in the difficult times that our love for the Lord strengthens us, comforts us, and brings us through. Love conquers all. Jesus demonstrated His love for us in the Garden of Gethsemane when He was about to be captured and He said, "Thy Will be done." (Matt. 26:42). Jesus showed His love for us while being beaten, and even while on the cross, as He sacrificed His life for us. Love is consistent.

Love God, even when you have sinned. You cannot hide your sin from the Lord. He is omniscient (all-knowing); He already knows you sinned. He is omnipresent; He was watching as you sinned. Do not try to hide and do not try to pretend it did not happen. Repent, ask the Lord to forgive you; stop running, do right, and love God sincerely. "Love shall cover a multitude of sins" (1 Pet. 4:8). God's unconditional love for you and your sincere love for Him will strengthen you against sin and keep you in right standing with Him.

God's love for us is incomprehensible to the natural mind. Yet, He desires that we "know the love of Christ, which passeth knowledge, that ye might be filled with all the fullness of God" (Eph. 3:19). God's love passes any knowledge or understanding we could have. Yet, the Lord loves us unconditionally. He will give us the strength, the spiritual gifts, and the boldness we need to do what He has called us to do when we receive His Love and love Him with all we are.

Loving the Lord pleases Him. We love the Lord when we do the following, simultaneously:

1) When we are righteous [in right standing with Him].
2) When we obey Him and trust Him.
3) When we serve Him and serve our neighbor.
4) When we love Him. and love our neighbor as ourselves.
5) When we forgive others and ourselves.
6) When we worship Him, praise Him, and thank Him.

*The Joy of the Lord is our strength!*

When pleasing the Lord is our number one priority, it brings the Lord Joy. "The Joy of the Lord is our strength" (Neh. 8:10). The more we please the Lord, the more joy we bring to Him. The more joy we bring to the Lord, the more strength we will gain to please Him even more. The joy of the

Lord is what strengthens us to carry out our assignment and ministry. The joy of the Lord is what strengthens us to be a credible witness. The joy of the Lord strengthens us to carry out works we would otherwise never be able to accomplish on our own. Choose to please the Lord in every thought, act and decision. Bring joy to the Lord and in return be strengthened to please the Lord even more.

## LOVE IS THE GREATEST GIFT

God is love, and He gave us the greatest gift of love when He sacrificed His Son so that He could dwell in us. The Holy Spirit in us enables us to love others unconditionally. Love is the principal thing, above all else. No matter how much money you donate to help the poor, or how much time you spend volunteering to help the poor, if you do not love the poor, in the eyes of the Lord, you have done nothing. The Word tells us, "Though I speak with the tongues of men and of angels, but have not love, I have become as sounding brass, or a tinkling cymbal. And though I have the gift of prophecy, and understand all mysteries and all knowledge, and though I have all faith, so that I could remove mountains, but have not love, I am nothing. And though I bestow all my goods to feed the poor, and though I give my body to be burned, but have not love, it profits me nothing (I Cor. 13:1–3).

"Love suffers long and is kind; love does not envy; love does not parade itself, is not arrogant; does not behave rudely, does not seek its own, is not easily provoked, keeps no account of evil does not rejoice in iniquity, but rejoices in the truth; bears all things, believes all things, hopes all things, endures all things. Love never fails" (I Cor. 13:4–8a).

Everything we do, we must do it with love.

## LOVE YOUR BROTHER

Your neighbor is your brother. Your neighbor or brother is whomever you have a conversation with. It is everyone around you, every person with whom you come in contact. "And the second is like, namely this, Thou shalt love thy neighbor as thyself. There is none other commandment greater than these" (Mark 12:31).

While on the cross, Jesus demonstrated His unconditional love for mankind. First by asking the Father to forgive those who were carrying out His crucifixion, then by telling His fellow neighbor that, today he would be with Jesus in Paradise. Jesus did not look at what the people yelling from the ground were saying or what they were doing. His love was unconditional. We must also love our brother, unconditionally, as the Lord commands. "Beloved, let us love one another: for love is of God, and everyone that loveth is born of God, and knoweth God. He that loveth not, knoweth not God; for **God is love**" (1 John 4:7–8). Love is the principal thing because love is of God, and God is love.

One of the greatest lessons I learned from my mother was that when someone was acting ugly, I was to "look beyond their fault and see their need." This is a powerful concept that works to keep your

*Look beyond their fault and see their need.*

heart pure; it keeps you in a state of ministry. Rather than focusing on what the person is saying or doing, the focus is on the state the person is in; they are in a dark and ugly place at that moment. Consider that you would not want to be in such a dark and ugly state or condition. Seeing their dark state can cause you to have compassion for them and to pray for them. Amid them being ugly towards you, pray for them. Do not pray aloud; do not move your lips. Pray in your heart. Praying for someone who mistreats you causes your prayer to bless them, and it blesses you; it keeps your heart pure.

Love for the Lord, and love for your brother, can only stem from a pure heart. A pure heart loves unconditionally. A pure heart looks beyond a person's fault and sees their need. Once you can see a person's need, you can pray for your brother. A pure heart allows you to see.

The Word even tells us to love our enemies. "Love your enemies, bless them that curse you, do good to them that hate you, and pray for them which despitefully use you, and persecute you" (Matt. 5:43–45). Initially, this will seem to be an impossible task. However tough, it is what we must do. This is why having a pure heart is essential. Looking beyond a person's fault to see their need will keep your heart pure. A pure heart will keep you in a state of ministry, such that you will be able to see the person's need and pray for them; pray for your enemies.

Keep your heart pure; it is essential to please the Lord. The Lord treasures a pure heart. "Blessed are the pure in heart: for they shall see God" (Matt. 5:8). Often, how we regard a person is based on their financial status, their education, their position in life, and how many "toys" they have. None of that matters to the Lord. The

*The Lord looketh on the heart.*

Lord looks at the heart. "The LORD seeth not as man seeth; for man looketh on the outward appearance, but the LORD looketh on the heart" (1 Sam. 16:7). In your prayer time, ask the Lord to give you a pure heart. Ask the Lord to search your heart and remove anything

*The heart fuels the thoughts of the mind.*

that does not please Him. "Those things which proceed out of the mouth come forth from the heart; and they defile the man. For out of the heart proceed evil thoughts, murders, adulteries, fornications, thefts, false witness, blasphemies" (Matt. 15:18–19). The heart fuels the thoughts of the mind. A pure heart is essential to loving your brother, to praying for your enemies, and to pleasing God.

## We ARE Our Brother's Keeper

Love is an action verb; you must demonstrate your love. Simply saying we love our brother is empty. If we are not actively doing something to help someone <u>outside of our family</u>, our words ring hollow.

How important is it to God for you to love your brother? This passage makes it clear: "In this the children of God are manifest, and the children of the devil: whosoever doeth not righteousness is not of God, **neither he that loveth not his brother**" (I John 3:10).

We must love those in need. Each of us can do something to help someone in need. There are people all around us who are in need, and their need could be anything. Your first thought may be for people who are in need of food or clothes, and if you can help in that area, great. Perhaps there are people around you who need to learn to read or who need a mentor. Perhaps a teen wants to go to college but has no one to point them in the right direction. The needs of families around us are great. Whether you help a person directly or volunteer through a nonprofit organization, do all you can to demonstrate your love for your brother. Ask the Lord to show you whom to help, and how to help. Whatever help you give, give it with love.

We must love those who hurt us. Remember, at all times, you must remain in right standing with the Lord. Remember, also, that you need Jesus more than you need anybody! Never let the actions of anyone cause you to get off track with the Lord. When someone hurts you, look beyond their fault and see their need. Often when a person hurts another, they are acting out of their own pain. Pray for them. Pray that the source of their pain will go away. Pray that the Lord will show them the error of their way. Pray that the Lord will take away their stony heart and give them a heart of flesh. Praying for those who hurt you will be a blessing to them <u>and</u> to you. Praying for those who hurt you will cause you to become stronger, spiritually.

We must love those who are not saved and point them to the Lord, for He has "given to us the ministry of reconciliation" (2 Cor. 5:18). We are here to lead our neighbor to Christ. We have opportunities every day to be a credible witness to our brother. Whether we pray the prayer of salvation with them, tell them that Jesus loves them, or perhaps just give words of encouragement, we must at least do something.

Let the words of your mouth minister and encourage, not hurt or offend. Do your part to be a credible witness. You may not be the one who prays the prayer of salvation with them. Perhaps God will send someone else along to handle that part when the person is ready. "Some plant, some water, but God

*Let the words of your mouth minister...*

gives the increase" (1 Cor. 3:6). Whatever your role along the person's journey, ensure that you bless the Lord in doing your part to demonstrate love for your brother.

We must serve our brother. We demonstrate love through our service to others. The more you serve your brother, the less you will focus on your own challenges. The less you focus on your own challenges, the more peace you will have and the more available you will be to the Lord. Your challenges will diminish in your sight with the fulfillment you receive through serving others. No matter what your personal challenges are, love and serve your brother. Jesus loved even while on the cross. Identify someone or some organization where you can volunteer your support. Render your time and demonstrate your love through service to your brother.

*In your patience possess ye your souls.*

We must be patient with our brother. Others may not change or grow at the pace we want them to grow. We did not grow at the rate those who were helping us wanted either. Patience is a virtue. Patience is one of the fruits of the Spirit, referred to as long-suffering, which means to suffer a long time. Being patient with others and being patient with how God is moving in your life is critical to your own spiritual growth. "In your patience possess ye your souls" (Luke 21:19).

Serve and love, regardless of what is going on in your personal life. Find fulfillment in loving and serving your brother. "We know that we have passed from death to life, because we love the brethren. He that loveth not his brother abideth in death" (1 John 3:14).

## BECOME SINGLE AND COMPLETE IN JESUS

We can be married or unmarried, but in either case, we must be single. In this case, single means complete in Jesus. As a Christian, you are to be whole and complete in Jesus. Many people spend years looking for that right person who will complete them. I personally know someone who has been divorced four times. When you look for something or someone in the natural to complete you, you will miss the mark every time. No person or thing can complete you.

You are spirit, and only Jesus' Holy Spirit can complete you. In Jesus dwells the fullness of everything you need. "And ye are complete in Him, which is the head of all principality and power" (Col. 2:10). You are complete in Jesus. Only Jesus can make you whole. Not a person. Not a thing. Not a title or position. Not money, big houses, or fancy stuff. "No bed, no bottle and no buzz can bring you the joy of Jesus." Jesus and only Jesus can make you whole and complete. You are a self-contained, single unit, able to operate in the things the Lord has called you to do through the indwelling power of the blessed Holy Spirit.

*No bed, no bottle and no buzz can bring you the joy of Jesus!*

People who are looking to others to complete them always end up disappointed with a relationship that did not give them what they expected. That is because a human cannot complete another human. We expect from others what they cannot give; this leaves us disappointed again, and again. We are complete in Jesus and in Jesus alone.

Surround yourself with other single people who recognize that they are complete in Jesus. Rather than being needy or draining on the relationship, two complete people will be able to strengthen and encourage each other. "Iron sharpens iron" (Prov. 27:17); therefore, you will each be able to keep the other lifted up, focused, in the Will of God, motivated, and purposely serving the Lord.

## SACRIFICE.

Sacrifice is an innate part of the Christian walk. Jesus sacrificed and paid the ultimate price, for us. The beauty is, though Jesus' sacrifice seemed harsh and even brutal at the time, it was for a far greater good. Jesus knew His sacrifice was for a greater good, and knowing that strengthened Him to finish. As Christ-like ones, each of us will also have to sacrifice. The beauty in our sacrifice is that it will also be for the greater good. Knowing that greater good will strengthen you to finish.

You will have to give up the habits and activities you used to do in the world. You will have to give up certain movies and TV shows with ungodly content. You will have to give up carnal friends and those who choose to stay in the world; at least give up close relations with them. You may even have to give up your current employment for something less glamorous or with a lower salary. Should the Lord orchestrate such a move, there is something you must learn and do in this new position. What you must learn and do will be for your spiritual growth, for the benefit of another, and to the glory of the Lord.

God will assuredly require you to sacrifice something, many different times, and in many different areas. "Whosoever will come after me, let him deny himself, take up his cross, and follow me" (Mark 8:34).

Your sacrifice will be unique to you and to your journey. Know that a relationship with the Lord requires your sacrifice. You will have to give up your own will and always put the Will of the Father before your will. "For you are bought with a price: therefore, glorify God in your body, and in your spirit, which are God's" (1 Cor. 6:20). Yes, God gave us free will, but He wants us to choose to do His Will. He has plans for you that are far greater than what you can do or imagine on your own.

Walking with the Lord is refreshing, therapeutic, and fulfilling. When you know in your heart that the Lord has given you a burden for a work He wants you to do, when you sense that the Lord is calling you to fulfill a purpose or to carry out an assignment, the sacrifice will be minuscule to you. It will not even feel like it is a sacrifice; rather, it will be freeing to you. You will gladly give up worldly, meaningless things to walk in the greater things of God. Walking in your assignment will be the most fulfilling thing you have ever done.

## BE SET APART

There are times when you will have to separate yourself. Take time alone with the Lord for guidance, direction, and wisdom. Daily, the world bombards us with sights and sounds. Take time to refresh yourself in the Word, whether you go away somewhere or take a sabbatical at home. I suggest including multiple sabbaticals at home so you can take time for reflection and direction any time you need. You may find that you need a prolonged time of separation, maybe months or years. When this occurs, the Lord is calling you away from certain people and activities to prepare you for His use. The purpose of the time of separation

*When this occurs, the Lord is calling you away from certain people and activities to prepare you for His use.*

is to draw you nearer to the Lord, for only He can guide you to, and through, your assignment. Ask Him every question you can think of. Ask Him to show you what to do and how to do it. Ask Him to guide your mind, your thoughts, and your words. Allow Him to lead you by the indwelling power of the Holy Spirit. The Holy Spirit is your director, your enabler, and your guide.

## BE CONTENT

We are to be content in whatsoever state we are in (Phil. 4:11). Whatever the condition or circumstance, we are to be content. If we keep our focus on the spiritual things of God, our circumstances will have little or no significance in relation to our peace. No matter what the circumstances are, we **can** be content if we continuously follow the instructions of the Lord. God tells us to keep our eyes on Him and not on our circumstances. It is only when we are content and at peace that we can truly focus on what God would have us to do. His peace is greater than your circumstance.

When you go through your period of sacrifice, you may not have the money you used to have. Just tighten the belt, become a solid financial steward, and press forward, thanking God for what you do have. You may not have the friends you use to have; they may think you have now become a "holy roller." They may not be able to relate to you anymore because they are still in the world. They may talk about you, talk against you and even turn against you. "If you were in the world, the world would love his own; but because you are not of the world, but I have chosen you out of the world, therefore the world hateth you" (John 15:19).

Remind yourself, "I need Jesus more than I need anybody breathing!" Then press forward, thanking God for your relationship with Him.

Your sacrifice will seem minuscule in comparison to the fulfillment you receive in serving the Lord. Things may not go the way you want them to go. You may not have your old friends; consider that a blessing, for God has better relationships in store. Things may not progress the way you thought they would, or as fast as you thought they should, but be sure you are in the Will of God and press forward, thanking God for His grace and mercy.

Be content no matter what your situation is. "Be anxious for nothing; but in everything with prayer and supplication with thanksgiving let your requests be made known unto God" (Phil. 4:6). Talk with the Lord. Share your concerns with the Lord. The Lord knows you, and He knows what you need. He knows your concerns. He just wants to hear from you. The Lord knows what He called you to do, and He knows what you need to do it. He will lead you, guide you, and provide you with everything you need. Talk with Him. Obey Him. Trust Him.

**Your sacrifice and obedience will bring the reward of fulfillment and purpose that money cannot buy.**

## BEAR FRUIT

When we are filled with the indwelling power of the Holy Spirit, submitted to the leading of the Holy Spirit, and have become matured in our Christian walk, we will bear the fruit of the Spirit. Our spiritual growth and maturity in the Lord will manifest in the natural through our character, our conversation, our behavior, and even our thoughts — all of which must glorify the Lord and edify those we encounter. All that we say and all that we do must emanate from the fruit of the Spirit. We will manifest the fruit of the Spirit in our daily lives, with the fruit of the Spirit visible to others. That is why the Lord says, "Wherefore, by their fruits ye shall know them" (Matt. 7:20).

"But the fruit of the Spirit is **love, joy, peace, longsuffering, gentleness, goodness and faith, meekness, and temperance...**" (Gal. 5:22–23).

<u>Love</u> is the first and greatest commandment. "Love God with all your heart, and with all your soul, and with all your mind" (Matt. 22:37). "Love your neighbor as yourself" (Matt. 22:39). Love for the Lord and love for your brother can only stem from a pure heart. A pure heart loves unconditionally. A pure heart looks beyond the fault and sees the need and enables one therefore to pray for his brother. As discussed earlier in this chapter, love is the principal thing, because love is of God, and God is love. "Beloved, let us love one another: for love is of God, and every one that loveth is born of God, and knoweth God. He that loveth not, knoweth not God; for God is love" (1 John 4:7–8).

The greatest demonstration of love we can show is when we put another's spiritual welfare as our priority, even to our own sacrifice. This very powerful testament requires both a pure and a committed heart. When we think of our neighbor as being anyone in our sphere of influence, this becomes an awesome task. The only way we can be effective in laying down our life for our friends is to follow the example Christ gave and love unconditionally. We must love, regardless of whether they love you in return. Love when you are mistreated. Guard your heart that you do not react to unkind treatment. Guard your heart, for out of it come the issues of life. <u>Whatever is truly in your heart will come out when tested.</u>

<u>Joy</u> is a state of being. Joy is not situational, like happiness. We are happy at our birthday party, or when we get a big promotion, or when we take a vacation; happiness is situational. Joy is a state of being; it is consistent. We have joy in good times and bad. We have joy when the storms of life are raging and when the sun shines gently on our face. We have joy with family and friends, as well as when there is no one around. Joy comes only from the Lord. When we are in the Will of God, operating in our spiritual gifts, and carrying out our assignment, joy will overflow. Joy manifests with spiritual maturity as a fruit of the Spirit.

Remember, the joy of the Lord is your strength (Neh. 8:10). When your obedience and steadfastness please the Lord, it brings Him joy. His joy is your strength. His joy strengthens you to go further, to overcome, and to continue to press toward the mark.

Peace is internal. No matter what type of chaos or drama may be going on around you, you can still have peace. Peace is internal. It is a state of being. The Word says, "Thou will keep him in perfect peace, whose mind is stayed on thee, because he trusts in thee" (Is. 26:3). Keep Jesus in mind and at the forefront of your thoughts all day, every day, no matter what is going on around you. Jesus is the Prince of Peace (Is. 9:6). When we are in Jesus and He is in us, no matter what is going on around us, we can be in peace.

Peace is the barometer through which we gauge whether we are in the Will of God. When anxiety abounds, and worry is present, check your position in the Will of God. The Lord promises us peace that passes understanding when we are in the center of His will. "And, the peace of God, which passes understanding, shall keep your hearts and minds through Christ Jesus" (Phil. 4:7). Because the Prince of Peace will keep your heart and mind, you can stay in a state of peace.

Your life should be peaceful; your home should be peaceful. Drama is of the world. It is not a fruit of the Spirit and should not be a part of your life. To stay in peace, you must bring peace and speak peace into every situation and every conversation. Keep your mind on things above and not beneath. Do not worry about things of this world; put your affection on the things of God. "Set your affection on things above, not on things on the earth" (Col. 3:2).

When we think on things that are true, honest, just, pure, lovely, and of good report, we will stay in peace (Phil. 4:8). When we seek first the Kingdom of God, pray without ceasing and pray for those who persecute us, we can trust that we will continually be at peace. When we keep our mind on the things of God and on His goodness, His mercy, and His grace, and when we seek His face, His love, and His guidance, and when we thank Him for His blessings, His protection, and His favor, and when His praise is continually in our mouth, we cannot help but be in perfect peace.

Longsuffering is having enduring patience with that hardheaded child, or that stubborn spouse, or that envious sibling, or that annoying co-worker and demanding boss. Longsuffering means to suffer a long time. The Lord suffered long with us before we knew Him. Jesus suffered long with us even after we knew Him and before we grew up into Him. We may even suffer long through health challenges or illness. That is a part of life; things happen. The key is to remember who you are and whose you are: a child of the Most-High God, heir to the Throne of Grace! "Let patience have her perfect work, that ye may be perfect and entire, wanting nothing." (James 1:4). Have patience with others, remembering the patience the Lord has with you. Have patience amid the trials, as you follow the Lord leading you through it. Have patience with the Lord, for His timing is perfect. "In your patience possess ye your soul" (Luke 21:19).

*In your patience possess ye your soul.*

Gentleness is a reflection of the heart. We are to have a pure heart. A pure heart is a gentle heart. A pure heart is visible to others because it shines through our actions and words. When we are gentle, we have a calming presence and a pleasant disposition. It is easy to have a kind word or a ministering word for someone, whether a friend or a stranger. A pure and gentle heart reflects our attitude about ourselves, our attitude towards others, and our attitude toward the Lord.

<u>Goodness and Faith</u>. Goodness is acting out of love and doing the right thing because it is the right thing to do. This happens when we love, care, are kind and have faith that all things work together for our good. Goodness is caring for others when they do not know how to care for themselves. Goodness is being kind, just because. It is doing kind things both planned and spontaneously. Goodness is doing without thought of reward, knowing that God sees.

<u>Meekness</u> is power under control. Meekness is having the power to destroy, punish, or humiliate, but you choose not to. Meekness is seeing others flair and boast, while you maintain a noble posture. Meekness knows you can do something greater or better than others, whether physically, intellectually, or financially, but you do it quietly and modestly, often unseen.

<u>Temperance</u> is self-control. Temperance possesses your reins, controls your flesh. It is staying focused and not letting the actions of others throw you off course. Temperance is controlling your actions and reactions while not letting others push your button. Temperance sustains you to not be provoked to act in a way that does not glorify the Lord. Temperance makes you consistent in your conduct and your character. Temperance is remaining calm amid chaos.

When we manifest the fruit of the Spirit, we will also manifest righteousness. "For the fruit of the Spirit is in all goodness, and righteousness and truth" (Eph. 5:9).

Bearing fruit of the Spirit is the manifestation of spiritual maturity. The fruit of the Spirit empowers us to edify others as a credible witness and to lead others to Christ as a minister of reconciliation. The fruit of the Spirit prospers us in our assignment to the glory and honor of the Lord. "Wherefore by their fruits ye shall know them" (Matt. 7:20).

*Chapter 7*

# WALK IN YOUR CALLING

The journey to your calling is a spiritual journey. It is a journey of spiritual maturity where you have allowed the Lord to purge, prune, and perfect you. It is a journey filled with trials, tribulations, and triumphs. You triumph because you are empowered by the Holy Spirit to overcome. You have learned to embrace the trials. You recognize the trials as learning experiences that build your trust in God and God's trust in you. You understand that each trial is God's spiritual barbell to exercise your faith and strengthen you. You know that each trial presents a test you must pass before God can move you to the next level of spiritual purpose.

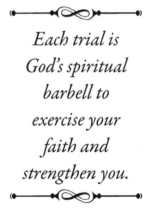

*Each trial is God's spiritual barbell to exercise your faith and strengthen you.*

Throughout the journey, you have allowed the Lord to lead you and use you. You walk in your spiritual gifts, knowing the gifts enable you to walk this walk. You learned to trust the Lord because of His faithfulness to you. Out of His faithfulness, you learned to trust; you obey, today. The journey is your faith in action; it reveals your willingness to fight the good fight. You fight recognizing that the battle is not yours, but it is the Lord's. You recognize that you are in spiritual warfare and you have put on the whole armor of God. You find comfort in knowing that the Lord will do the work through you. You love God and you love your brother, and you demonstrate your love in action. You let your words minister to your brother in love. You have accepted that God has set you apart; you are single — whole and complete in Jesus. You recognize that you need Jesus more than you need anybody, period. You have a love for the Lord that is greater than your love for anyone or anything. You sacrifice worldly things for the greater things of God. You have a holy boldness for the things of the Word and a righteous indignation for things of the world. You are a vessel of the Lord and bear the fruit of the Spirit. You find joy and fulfillment in the work and the Will of the Lord.

## RECEIVE THE DESIRES OF YOUR HEART

No one ever starts out knowing what the Lord wants him or her to do. It is when we obey then gain trust, and let Him lead, guide, perfect, and mature us daily, that we stay on course. As we journey with the Lord, we will find ourselves in the place, position, and purpose He ordained for us.

The Word tells us, "Delight thyself also in the Lord: and He shall give you the desires of your heart" (Ps. 37:4). Often people interpret this to say God will give you whatever you desire. Some think it means that whatever we desire, we can ask the Lord for it and He will give it to us. I do not agree. I believe the meaning of this Scripture is much different. First, this is another of those Scriptures that has a promise with a condition:

- Promise: He shall give you the desires of your heart.
- Condition: Delight thyself in the Lord.

Additionally, we must satisfy the condition: delight ourselves in the Lord. When we find joy and fulfillment in serving the Lord, obeying the Lord, trusting the Lord, pleasing the Lord, allowing the Lord to use us, allowing the Holy Spirit to lead us, loving the Lord and our brother, and leading others to the Lord, we delight ourselves in the Lord.

The more you delight yourself in the Lord, the more you will want to delight yourself in Him, for there is fulfillment in serving the Lord. There is fulfillment in being a vessel used by the Lord.

The promise part of this Scripture says He shall give you the desires of your heart. The Lord will give you THE DESIRE. It is the Lord's desire for you. It is the work the Lord sent you to this earth to do. The Lord will cause you to desire to do the work He purposed for you. He will plant the desire in your heart for the work of your calling. He gives you the calling by planting the desire to do the work in your heart. When the Lord gives you the desire, He is placing a calling on your life. This does not mean you are going to become an ordained minister of the Gospel or a preacher in the pulpit. It simply means the Lord has given you a calling to do the specific work He purposed for you. Receiving the desires of your heart is receiving the desire, and accepting the call, to do the work the Lord created you to do. It is a work He wants to do through you.

## REMAIN IN SPIRITUAL PERCEPTION

Just as I was in spiritual perception in 2008, when the Lord caused me to discern that there was a pervasive problem regarding mass incarceration of black males, be perceptive and discerning as to what the Lord is showing you. I saw the problem spiritually while looking at natural men.

As with me, you may not know what the problem is right away. You may not know what you can or should do. I did not realize it at the time, but this was the beginning of the Lord planting the desire in my heart to protect His children from the institutional rise in mass incarcerations.

It was the prison visit in July of 2010 with Leadership Maryland to the maximum-security prison in Cumberland, Maryland, when I entered one of the prison cells and heard the clink of that cell door closing, that I knew THIS was the work the Lord was drawing me to. In October 2010, after an emotional outbreak from the entire class to the question, "How did the prison visit impact you?" I knew WHAT the Lord wanted me to do: to stem the flow of youth toward the historic oppression of the prison system and to strengthen them toward a productive path forward.

The Lord had planted the seed of desire in my heart to do His Will to address the challenges of mass incarceration. This was God putting His Calling on my life; He was giving me the assignment of The Clarion Call.

Whatever your calling, only the Lord can show you what it is, prepare you for it, and strengthen you to do it. And, whatever your calling is, it will be something far greater than you could ever do on your own. It is a work that the Lord must do, and He wants to do it through you.

The vision the Lord shows you will be larger than what you can do on your own, and it will not make sense to your natural mind. However, you will know spiritually that it is something the Lord wants you to do. Follow the leading of the Lord, even if it does not seem to make sense. The Word says, "But the natural man receiveth not the things of the Spirit of God: for they are foolishness to him: neither can he know them, because they are spiritually discerned" (1 Cor. 2:14). You may not understand what the Lord means or intends in the beginning because the natural mind cannot comprehend the spiritual things of God. The Holy Spirit will illuminate the assignment to you. Ask the Lord to show you what to do. Start to take small steps in doing the things you know to do now.

Ask the Lord questions. Ask Him to show you how to do this work or that task. Ask Him to show you whom to go to, whom to approach, etc. Ask Him to show you how to apply Scripture He gives you. For example, one of the Scriptures He gave me was "Loose the bands of wickedness" (Isa. 58:6). I asked Him what IS the wickedness? What are the bands? And, how do you loosen them? I ended up with nine pages of instructions. The Lord loves it when we ask Him spiritual questions. "What things soever you desire, when you pray, believe you receive them and you shall have them" (Mark 11:24). Remember, this means whatever QUESTIONS you desire the Lord to answer; ask and you shall have the answer. Your questions should be for wisdom, guidance, and direction. His answers are the "things" He will so readily give us when we pray.

Your spiritual discernment will enable you to perceive what the Lord wants you to do. You will discern gradually what it is you must do to carry out your assignment. The Holy Spirit will lead, guide, and direct you daily along your journey.

That is why obedience and trust are so critical. God may show you a big picture of the work you are to do, but you need the Holy Spirit to lead you through the details of how to get started. You need the Holy Spirit to lead you through the tests and trials. Obey whatever the Lord leads you to do, period. Obey when you do not understand. Obey when it hurts. Obey when it means you must sacrifice. Obedience births trust.

## "BUT I KNOW NOTHING ABOUT THIS TOPIC!"

When the Lord plants the desire in your heart to do a certain task, whether it makes sense to your natural mind is irrelevant. What is relevant is your obedience.

Here are three examples of tasks the Lord told me to do that made no sense to my natural mind. Also, I had no experience in any of the task areas. None. But I knew the tasks were from God, and I knew it was work I was to carry out.

1. In 2008, the Lord had sensitized me that something was wrong regarding males in the black community. I was in a state of perception like never before. I did not realize it then, but this was the Lord planting the seed in my heart to do His Will and His work in this area. In 2009, the perception intensified. In 2010, He orchestrated for me to be in Leadership Maryland and I visited a prison for the first time in my life. The visit was complete with an intimate tour of a massive maximum-security prison. In October, at the end of the Leadership Maryland Class of 2010, my entire class was moved by my question: "How did the prison visit impact you?" With tears and deep sorrow, all 52 members of my class were emotionally impacted. The class rallied behind my charge to them that, "Whenever a discussion takes place that evokes an emotion in nearly every person in the room, we witness the genesis of an assignment — a clarion call to action." The class accepted my charge to them and began naming my charge The Clarion Call.

At the end of 2010, the Lord told me to start a nonprofit. I knew nothing about nonprofits. I had never even volunteered at a nonprofit, other than my church. The Lord also let me know the nonprofit was to focus on prison-prevention and on disrupting the school-to-prison pipeline. I knew nothing about prisons or pipelines. I did not know the difference between a jail and a prison, nor could I tell you where one was located. I knew nothing about mass incarceration or collateral consequences. I had never contemplated starting a nonprofit. Yet, I knew this was the Lord.

In 2011, I took the entire year off from working my business and did nothing but research. I knew nothing about this new arena of prisons and mass incarceration; I had to research and study. At the end of a full year of research, in December 2011, I filed incorporation papers for The Clarion Call. I wrote my own nonprofit application and filed for nonprofit status with the IRS; I had never filed for nonprofit status before. The IRS approved my 501(c)(3) determination of nonprofit status within 30 days, likely a record. In April 2012, I launched The Clarion Call. Our mission is to disrupt the prison pipeline. Visit our website at www.TheClarionCall.info.

2.  In 2012, the Lord told me to launch a television show for The Clarion Call. He said we were to have showcase shows and issue shows. I knew absolutely nothing about doing a TV show. However, a few years earlier, the Lord had orchestrated for me to be on the board of directors for Prince George's Community Television, the county cable TV station. The president of the TV studio asked another board member to work with me on the show. A volunteer at the studio, whom I knew from my former church, also worked with me to get the show started. The volunteer suggested the concept of creating our set design. The board member wrote my first script. They helped me understand the lingo of the TV production world. The Lord led me to select the perfect music. My goddaughter created a short but impactful video for the opening of each show. And the Lord led me to readily identify guests who were eager to participate in this novice's TV show.

As of this writing, we have produced 65 episodes of *The Clarion Call* TV Show. Our showcase shows have hosted over 20 nonprofits to highlight their work. We have also featured young entrepreneurs and outstanding student leaders. Our issue shows feature subject-matter experts in panel discussions that delve into mass incarceration, police-community relations, domestic violence, spiritual grounding, behavioral health, fatherhood, homeless youth, mentoring, and more. We have hosted representatives from Congress, state delegates, County Chamber of Commerce, Sheriff's Department, chaplain of the county jail, county agencies, authors, and more. Anyone can view our shows on our website or our YouTube channel.

3. The Lord told me to write this book. I knew absolutely nothing about writing a book. I had never contemplated writing a book. I was working on multiple projects at the time and did not see how I could fit in writing a book. I asked the Lord, "HOW do I write the book?" The Lord said, "Arise early, at 5." The Lord gave me the title of this book. I had no idea what to write. I said to the Lord, "Lord, I have nothing to tell the people; I ask You to write the book through me." I began to receive an outpouring of topics, points, phrases and ideas. They would come so frequently and rapidly that I would always have a writing pad with me. Throughout the day, wherever I was, I would jot down every topic or thought. I organized what seemed like random topics and thoughts into groups. The groups seemed to have a sequence to them for what should be first or last. I put the groups in order. I began to name the groups which became the names of the chapters in the book. Under those, were subheadings in each chapter. The list of chapter titles with subheadings became my table of contents, which served as the outline for me to follow as I wrote. This meant the entire book was outlined from front to back prior to me writing the first sentence. Every morning, I awoke at 5:00 am, and propped myself up in the bed with my laptop in my lap. I wrote every

day, Sunday mornings before church 1.5 hours. Other days averaging 2–3 hours a day, but when there was a heavy snow with school and government closings, I would write 5 hours straight; this occurred on three occasions. I wrote every day for six months forming the entire first draft of this book in bed. Though I had never dealt with writing a book, I have lots of experience writing and editing large documents, specifically government proposals. It was still not easy, though, because I knew if the Lord told me to write the book, the Lord wanted the reader to hear Him, not me. He wanted readers to hear His guidance and faithfulness throughout my personal trials, tests, and triumphs. I pray you hear the Lord as you read this book.

## My "Instructions" from the Lord.

Seven years after the Lord initially planted the seed of desire in my heart to do the work of prison-prevention through The Clarion Call, He gave me instructions to further the assignment. As I was reading Scripture during morning devotion, a certain Scripture flashed at me. Of course, this meant the Lord was bringing my attention to the Scripture to DO something. (It was that flashing thing again!) The Lord used the same Scripture as when I created the "Repairer of the Breach" presentation for Pastor Cherry, Isaiah 58, except this time the Scripture was verse Isaiah 58:6 only. The Lord told me, "These are your Instructions" for The Clarion Call.

I wrote the Scripture down; there were four tasks in the Scripture as my "Instructions." These "instructions" made no sense to my natural mind. I prayed and asked the Lord to show me what each word meant in each of the four tasks within the Scripture. I also asked Him to show me what it was He wanted me to do. How was I to do the work? I asked Him to do the work through me. I studied each word, and then I cross-referenced the Scripture to other passages listed with it. I sought the Lord through every passage to show me what it meant and what He wanted me to carry out in this assignment.

It took months of study and prayer before I was able to translate four short passages into nine pages of action items for implementation of the instructions. It was a mighty work that only the Lord could do.

The Lord has heard the cry of His people, and in this area, He has called me to be a voice for those who have no voice — to love the people and cause them to see themselves as God sees them; to enlighten the people of the systemic challenges amassed against them; to engage the people in choosing life; to encourage the people to fight the good fight of faith. It is an awesome assignment and a powerful set of instructions. I am compelled to do this work. I am committed to this assignment and submitted to the Lord for Him to perform the instructions through me.

## RECOGNIZE, ACCEPT AND DECLARE YOUR CALLING

*It is a beautiful thing knowing the Lord trusts you to carry out a task on His behalf.*

Recognize what the Lord is leading you to do — that it is a spiritual work that must manifest in the natural. Your calling will always be a work you must do for the benefit of others. It will always be a work to help those in need. Recognize that the work is what the Lord wants done. Receive it and embrace it. It is a beautiful thing, knowing the Lord trusts you to carry out a task on His behalf.

Accept the work as your part of God's greater plan. Accept that God knows what to do and that He knows just how to do it. Accept that He has groomed you, perfected you, and matured you just for this assignment. He knows He can trust you because He was with you through every trial and tribulation along your journey. He knows you passed each test, and He, therefore, promoted you to the next level of spiritual purpose. Now, you are ready. The Lord is ready. There is a work to do in the earth realm, and the Lord chose you to perform it. He needs your heart, hands, feet, mind, mouth, and obedience to get it done. The Lord trusts you to continue to be faithful to Him. He will be faithful to you as you implement His work. He will not leave you. He will lead your every step.

Declare your calling. Do not think it; know it. Share it with those you feel led to share. Let others know the Lord has given you an assignment. Do not share details; speaking it with your mouth and believing in your heart is what is important. Seek counsel from your pastor. Gather other like-minded and spiritually mature people around you, as the Lord leads. "In the multitude of counsel there is safety" (Prov. 11:14). Seek wise counsel, yet stay on course and stay true to what the Lord told you to do. While the counsel of others may present a different way to approach the task, never let their counsel change the task. The task came from the Lord; be committed to doing what the Lord said to do.

By obeying the Lord and allowing Him to lead me day by day, task by task, test by test, trial by trial, and year by year, He guided me, matured me, and strengthened me. He was preparing me for something I was not yet ready to handle. After many years and overcoming many trials, the Lord gave me my assignment of The Clarion Call to disrupt the prison pipeline. The more I diligently obeyed and followed as He led in developing the organization and carrying out the work of The Clarion Call, the Lord found me faithful, so He continues to lead and show me more of what He wants the organization to do. He has proven Himself faithful because He has found me faithful. I am more fulfilled doing the work of The Clarion Call than anything else I have ever done.

## CARRY OUT YOUR ASSIGNMENT

Whatever the Lord tells you to do, your obedience is most critical. Obedience births trust. Once you obey, you will see God work things out like you never thought possible. You will see the faithfulness of God, time after time. Experiencing that faithfulness of God will instill trust in your heart. You will develop an unshakable trust that assures you that no matter what He assigns you to do, you will be able to carry it out with the help of the Lord. You will know that the Holy Spirit will do the work through you.

Daily, ask the Lord to lead you in carrying out your assignment. Walk in your assignment. Be diligent and steadfast. Do not be slothful. The Word says we must "not be slothful in business but fervent in spirit, serving the Lord" (Rom. 12:11). People in need who are hurting are waiting for you to act. Do not take the assignment lightly. God has something HE wants done, and He has chosen to work through you to carry out the assignment. That is an honor and a privilege! Show gratitude by diligently working while it is day. Be diligent because while God is working through you, He is simultaneously working through others to orchestrate your works together for the greater good.

Remember the "wilderness experience"? You may have a season where the Lord takes you through "training ground" exercises. You may feel all alone, bewildered, and worn, but stay the course! These experiences will teach you things you need to know in your assignment. These experiences will strengthen you in areas where you are yet weak and will perfect you for your assignment. Do not begrudge the wilderness experiences. Be thankful for these experiences. Be thankful that your Heavenly Father loves you enough to prepare you for the journey that is yours.

The more faithful you are in following as the Lord leads, the more faithful the Lord will be in showing you how to do what He is leading you to do.

When we want the Lord to do something in our lives, we cannot wait around for Him to drop it in our lap. We cannot wait until we get all our ducks in a row before we act. The Holy Spirit is a helper, not the doer. The Holy Spirit will help YOU do the work. Do not wait until you see evidence that everything is in place; that would not require faith. Having faith that God will do what He said means we must act based on what He said to do, whether it makes sense to us or not. Most times, the things the Lord tells us to do will not make sense to the natural mind. That is the point. That is why having faith in the Lord and trusting Him at His Word are so important. We must trust that God will do what He said He will do.

*The Holy Spirit is a helper, not the doer.*

Be strong and very courageous in your assignment, knowing that the Lord is with you; He will do the work through you. Speak with holy boldness, allowing the Lord to speak through you. Have a righteous indignation towards the ways of the world, knowing the Lord will fight your battles. Be humble, and keep your heart pure, for it is not you who will do the work. Being prideful, boastful, or arrogant will leave you empty and void of effect. "God resists the proud but gives grace to the humble" (James 4:6).

Be a credible witness. You never know who is watching you. You cannot afford to cause someone to stumble because of your actions or conversation. There should be nothing in your life that offends the Word of God. Nothing in your conduct, activities, acquaintances, or possession should bring question to your character.

## BE AVAILABLE TO GOD

Always be available to the Lord to speak a ministering word to whomever may be before you. You never know when someone may approach you who needs to be comforted. You never know when your phone may ring, and someone needs to hear a word from the Lord. You never know when you will encounter someone who is angry and wants to lash out at you. If you are in a state of ministry, you will not take their comments personally. See their hurt and have the compassion to pray for them, even if you pray without speaking. You never know when an accident may occur right in front of you, and the injured person needs reassurance.

On the way to church one Sunday, while driving on the four-lane Washington Beltway, the car in front of me over-corrected and started to spin. I started praying. There was traffic in all four lanes going at least 55 miles per hour. The car spun across all four lanes and the front car in each lane stopped. Someone could have hit my car from the rear since I was sitting still on the Beltway. The spinning car went from the far-right lane to the far-left lane, spinning across all four lanes, then back across all four lanes before stopping off the highway on the shoulder of the road. I pulled off the road and jumped out of my car, shouting and praising the Lord for keeping that car from crashing and that no one was injured. I ran to the driver, who was stunned and frantic but otherwise unhurt. I praised the Lord before her. In a bold, preacher voice, I told her only the Lord protected her from crashing. Only the Lord protected her from another car hitting her. I told her to raise her hands and praise the Lord with me. I told her to thank the Lord for shielding her from an accident; she repeated everything I told her to say. I told her the Lord must have work for her to do, that the Lord spared her for a reason. I boldly told her to surrender her all to the Lord and ask Him what He wanted her to do. I was actually preaching to the young woman. I was preaching so loudly and boldly that my voice became hoarse. I continued to Sunday Service at church, thanking the Lord all the way.

Stay in a state of ministry, such that you can always be a credible witness. Your love for God and your love for your brother will enable you to remain in a state ready to pray at any moment. Live in a state of humility, always ready to be a vessel used by God. You never know when the Lord wants to speak to you or speak through you. Be ready to minister. Be ready to minister to whomever the Lord puts before you. Be grateful the Lord uses you. Be ready to be ministered to, as well. Remaining teachable ensures your growth.

## WHEN GOD PUSHES PAUSE

Expect your commitment to the work to be tested. Even after you have received and accepted your calling and are working the work of your assignment, opportunities for spiritual growth, through trials and tests, will continue to come. Sometimes the Lord will "push pause" and have us slow down or stop a project because He sees into a future that we cannot see. Below are two occasions when God pushed pause amid me carrying out a task He instructed me to do:

## HATCHER'S HAVEN FAMILY PROPERTY DEVELOPMENT

In 2008, I had been working diligently, along with one of my sister trustees, to have the civil engineers lay out different schematics for dividing the acreage into lots. We met with architects who showed us how many structures we could have on the property and what they would look like. We met with adjoining landowners determining if they wanted to partner in our project with their small lot. We were talking with investors about the financials for developing the property. We subsequently approved a particular lot design concept and were prepared to go to the county to officially record 23 lots, keeping some of the acreage in the family.

It was at that point that I stopped. I had been busy scheduling meetings, identifying new players; and now nothing. I didn't feel led to call anyone or do anything. This went on for a couple of months.

Then I asked the Lord why I was not working on the family acreage. No answer. A year went by. No activity. No answer. My siblings did not inquire why we weren't working on the project; no one questioned what was going on or not going on.

It was 18 months later that the Lord had me see why He pushed pause. The Lord knew the recession of 2008 and 2009 was coming. We didn't know that, but our omniscient, all-knowing God knew it. Taking our eight acres of land to the county and recording it as 23 lots was a huge step. Huge because the solid eight acres is considered raw land and is taxed as one huge chunk of undeveloped land for property tax purposes. Once we recorded the lot designs with the county, even though no dirt had been moved, property taxes would have been set on a per-lot basis rather than on raw land. That means instead of paying $8,000 per year in property taxes for the chunk of land, we would have paid $4,000 per year, per lot on 23 lots! That would normally have been fine moving forward in development our investors and bank on the team. But with the recession, no one was lending or investing in anything. Without our investors and bank, the family would never have been able to pay the property taxes on the recorded lots. We would have lost the land for property taxes. Thank God for pushing pause! In His infinite wisdom, He saw what we and our investors could not see. The Lord saved us from imminent failure and the loss of our family inheritance.

## THE CLARION CALL READING CAMPAIGN

From the outset of the organization, I felt we were to offer reading services to students and adults alike. Two years after Clarion launched, I added a "Coming Soon" notice to our marketing flyer touting the addition of a reading program. However, there were a couple of Clarion board members, including the chair, who disagreed with offering the reading program, stating that it would be a distraction to our work. He convinced other members that we were better off not doing the reading program. I was trying to support the board, so the reading program did not get launched.

A couple of years later, we started the year with a fantastic strategic planning session, led by a very capable facilitator. All the board members were excited with the prospects and fully embraced our plans for the year; the entire year was planned out. All board members signed a pledge of financial contribution for the year. Everyone was elated.

I did not call another board meeting. Not the next month, nor the next, nor the next. I did not reach out to the board, and the board did not reach out to me. I took that as a good sign. I felt that God had pushed pause for me, and He had also pushed pause for the board members. This let me know that God was doing something, though I knew not what. This lasted for 18 months. I still hosted the TV show. I still spoke at a few small events. I still answered the phone when patrons called for help, but none of the plans from the retreat were carried out. I did not know why God had pushed pause. I did not know what He wanted me to see or do.

In the spring of the following year, I had a challenging encounter with guests who were to be on the TV show. One member of the team was abrupt, demeaning, accusatory, demanding, and very disrespectful, all while I was planning to showcase their organization on the show. I was seriously contemplating not hosting them on the show at all. Then the Lord had me listen to a radio recording of the organization being interviewed by someone else. He then told me I needed to be just as genuine and enthusiastic as the radio host, when I hosted them on my TV show. With that, my whole attitude changed. I was determined to do my very best to showcase them and their work, regardless of how I felt treated. They were thrilled with the TV interview; I got smiles, hugs, and a big thank you.

This entire TV show scenario had been a test for me. I did not realize it was a test until after I had passed the test by doing an exceptional show for them. Yes, I could have canceled the show, feeling disrespected. I could have laid out justifiable reasons for canceling, but how would that have ministered to them and to my team? How would that have demonstrated my unconditional love? How would cancellation have blessed them or me? It was right after passing this test that the Lord released the pause button. We must pass the tests, and the tests will continue to come.

The next week, I was online and came across a reading program I had not heard of before. I was not looking for a reading program. I had not even thought about the reading program. I just came across a site that had a link to a new program. My eyes got big as saucers when I saw it! I got so excited with the features and flexibility of the program that I immediately began to play around with it online and loved it. Then I signed up for a 30-day trial. I told my daughter, and we both got moms to agree to try it free for 30 days with their child.

That was the beginning of the refresh of The Clarion Call. The Lord had pushed pause on me as well as other members of the board. However, when I reached out to board members, after 18 months, it was as if there were slow down at all. Now the reading program is the heart of the organization's program services. And, the way the Lord showed me how to implement the reading program will enable us to reach far more students than I originally envisioned. Within three months, we were already collaborating with two other organizations who loved our model and wanted to support our work by getting their members involved.

God had pushed pause because while the prior year strategic planning session was well done and everyone was elated with the plan, it was not complete; in fact, the plan was off-base. We were missing the reading program. The Lord had put on my heart from the beginning that Clarion was to have a reading program. At the time, I did not see how the reading program was to be organized, I just knew we were to have one. Yet, in trying to follow the guidance of the board chair, we got distracted with not doing a reading program at all. Rather we should have actively pursued establishing a reading program. "We ought to obey God rather than men" (Acts 5:29). Follow what the Lord says, rather than what man says.

Stay true to what the Lord shows you to do. Take counsel from your board or other leadership but be sure their counsel does not change the direction or path the Lord laid out for you. God tells us **what** to do. Advisors help show you **how** to do what God said. Never should counsel from advisors change your efforts from what God said. After 18 months of not meeting with the board, and after I passed the test with the TV show guest, the Lord opened another window of opportunity. He showed me the new reading program online. I instantly saw the entire vision for the reading program in detail. The reading program is now the centerpiece of Clarion's program services.

When God pushes pause, continue to do what you are led to do, but do not try to force your way forward to do what you think should happen — your expected end. Be patient. Be prayerful. Be obedient. When God pushes pause, it is because He is protecting you from something you cannot see right now. In my case, He was protecting the organization from getting off track. He is preparing you for what you cannot do right now and from what you cannot see right now. When God pushes pause, it is always for your good.

## PRESS TOWARD THE MARK

Warning: Do not get so comfortable in your work that you think you have the "hang of it." Do not get so comfortable in your spiritual growth and maturity that you think you have spiritually arrived, so you can now permit yourself to ease off morning devotions. Do not get so accustomed to the work that you get on automatic pilot in making decisions on your own. One of the worst things you can do is to think you have grown to the point you can handle the work on your own.

You still have an adversary called the devil. The adversary will still try to distract you from your work. He will still present other seemingly feasible options to you and try to persuade you to embrace them.

Once you are walking in your calling, you will need the Lord the most. You will have an even greater need for morning devotions. You will have an even greater need to pray for direction. You will never have the "hang of it." You will need to seek the Lord even more in planning and decision-making. Options that seem feasible are not the way the Holy Spirit leads. The Lord is precise and clear. Ask Him for wisdom and direction, and then obey.

Your journey is really the Lord's journey. Your journey is an assignment the Lord has given you to carry out for Him. You do not have the option of changing the work. You must stay true to the work assigned to you. Do not add to it; subtract from it or go in a different direction. The Lord knows what He wants to accomplish through this work, whether you know or not. You just need to stay focused on the assignment and do as He leads.

You must stay true to who the Lord called you to be. He has matured, strengthened, and prepared you for this work. He took you through trial after trial, and you passed test after test, just to get to the point of receiving your calling. Now is not time to change course. The tests will continue to come. Continuing to stay true to the assignment is itself a test. Continuing to seek the Lord for guidance is itself a test. Continuing to work expeditiously is a test. Do not delay or put off any of the work. No matter how large or difficult a task may appear, nothing is too hard for God. This is His work; you are simply the vessel He chose to use to get the work done.

The trials and tests will never stop. Consider that the assignment you have now could possibly be just the beginning of what the Lord wants you to do. While the work you are doing now may seem enormous to you, it is tiny to the Lord. He may have even greater things in store for you. Be diligent in your work for Him. Be steadfast in your devotion to Him. Be committed to carrying out all that the Lord has put on your heart. You never know — perhaps the best is yet to come.

## BE STEADFAST AND UNMOVABLE

> "Therefore, my beloved brethren, be ye steadfast, unmovable, always abounding in the work of the Lord, forasmuch as ye know that your labor is not in vain in the Lord" (I Cor. 15:58).

All that you are belongs to the Lord, submitted to Him as a Holy sacrifice, and used for His service. You must not think of your life as what you want for it, but rather, what does the Lord want for you and from your life? Seek the Will of God in every area of your life. You cannot follow what others may be doing; no matter how exciting it may appear. Take on the mind of Christ, that you knowingly walk fully in the Will of God.

Let no one dissuade you from doing what the Lord has put on your heart to do. Let no one come before the Lord. Remember, you need Jesus more than you need anybody, period! You have come a long way to get to the point of receiving your calling. Disdain the distractions, whether they be people, places or things.

Your journey is your faith in action. Fight the good fight. Remember that the battle is not yours; it is God's. It is He who will do the work. Put on the whole armor of God so you can stand against the wiles of the devil. And, after having done all, still stand. Love God, love your brother, and bear fruit of the Spirit. Thank God for your assignment and give yourself fully to doing the work.

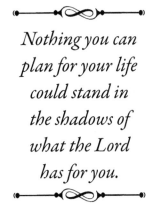

*Nothing you can plan for your life could stand in the shadows of what the Lord has for you.*

Nothing you can plan for your life could stand in the shadows of what the Lord has for you. Obey Him more, trust Him more, grow in Him more, live in Him more, and let Him live in you more, so that you can be used by Him more as He molds and shapes you into who He created you to be and to do the work He destined you to do.

Receive the desire of your heart! Accept the seed planted by the Lord. Embrace the work the Lord wants you to do to His glory and for the benefit of others. It is a beautiful thing when the Lord entrusts you to do His work, for His people.

May the joy of the Lord be your strength.
May the favor of the Lord prosper you.
May the grace of the Lord sustain you.
May the love of the Lord comfort you.
May the peace of the Lord be yours.

Walk in your calling, and let your light shine, in Jesus' name!

Janice Hatcher Liggins

# WHAT'S NEXT?

I encourage you to journal your experiences as you progress in your spiritual journey. Use the Table of Contents in this book to catalogue your journey.

We are also creating a Discussion Guide to accompany this book. Be sure to get the guide to assist you in chronicling your experiences and spiritual successes.

We will also host workshops, webinars and e-classes where we will delve deeper into the lessons we must learn in the seven progressions of your journey. Get your questions answered. Share your experiences. The workshops will encourage you, challenge you, and prayerfully inspire you along your own journey. Share how you experienced the seven progressions. Did you use the prayers? What challenges did you have and how did the Lord help you to overcome them? The workshops and webinars will be a perfect opportunity for you to glorify the Lord in His faithfulness to you and to let us know where you currently are along the *Journey to Your Calling*!

Visit our website, Facebook page or Instagram page to stay up to date for when we launch our Journey e-classes, webinars, workshops, book signings, and other events. Register for the webinars and events on our website www.JourneyToYourCalling.com.

Be sure to join our mailing list to keep updated on *Journey to Your Calling* activities and events.

May the blessings of the Lord be upon you.

Janice Hatcher Liggins

# Acknowledgements

THANK YOU! To each person who has affected my life over the years, thank you. Whether your presence in my life brought happiness or sadness, support or adversity, abundance or scarcity, I thank God for you, for I now know that the Lord used you to bless me. Those who brought happiness, support or abundance to my life, I thank the Lord for you, for the Lord used you to brighten my days and lighten my load. To those who brought sadness, adversity or scarcity, I thank the Lord for you, for the Lord used you to strengthen me and to draw me closer to Himself. Through the totality of my experiences, I have learned that "all things work together for good to them that love God, to them who are the called according to His purpose" (Rom. 8:28).

**THANK YOU TO PEOPLE WHO HELPED, NOT REALIZING IT...**

**Thank you, Jennifer, my dear sister** who, in 2004, asked me to write the words to the Armor Prayer so you could have them. You said, in your response to hearing me pray the prayer, "Janice! For the first time, I could actually SEE the armor! Do you think you can remember it? Do you think you can write it down for me?" Jennifer, thank you for asking me to write the prayer down. I had prayed that prayer for three years and had never written it down. Had you not asked, I may have never put the words of the prayer to paper. Now, because of your request, dozens of friends and family have received copies of the Armor prayer. I have also shared the Armor Prayer, in its entirety, in this book... thanks to you.

**Thank you, girl shopper** in the office supply store, for engaging in discussion with me inquiring of my assignment of The Clarion Call. When I mentioned that it is a calling for me, you asked me how I came into my calling. You said, "With your calling, did you pray and tell God that this is what you really wanted, and then He gave it to you?" Thank you for asking the question. It was only in answering your question, in that very moment, that I had ever thought about the process. It was only then that I realized just how I arrived at my assignment and how I received my calling. I have chronicled the journey to my calling in this book... thanks to you.

**Special Thank You To...**

**Thank you, Sister Toni Foxx,** for being the first reviewer and editor of this book. I was surprised you finished so quickly. I am grateful you found it a breeze to edit this work and categorized me as a good writer. I am thankful that you were blessed by the contents. I saw the first edited draft of my first book... thanks to you.

**Thank you, Rev. Diana P. Cherry,** for being willing to review the manuscript and write the foreword for this book. I am humbled and truly grateful for your glowing review of this work. I am even more grateful that your feedback confirmed that the book is a guide or roadmap for all who want to seek and find God's plan, purpose and Will for their lives. You confirmed what the Lord showed me. I thoroughly appreciate your feedback. I have finished this work... thanks to You.

**Most importantly… thank you, Heavenly Father,** for the assignment to write this book. Thank you for being the author and finisher of this work. Thank you for my life experiences, the happy ones and the difficult ones, for through them I learned of your faithfulness to me. Thank you for the blessings and the tribulations, for you used them to strengthen me and to grow me up into you. Thank you for orchestrating my path throughout the journey to my calling. Thank you for using me to write this book, working through me by the indwelling power of your blessed Holy Spirit. May you be glorified, and all who read it be edified, in the name of Jesus. I have completed your assignment to me to write this book… thanks to You.

With enduring gratitude,

Janice Hatcher Liggins

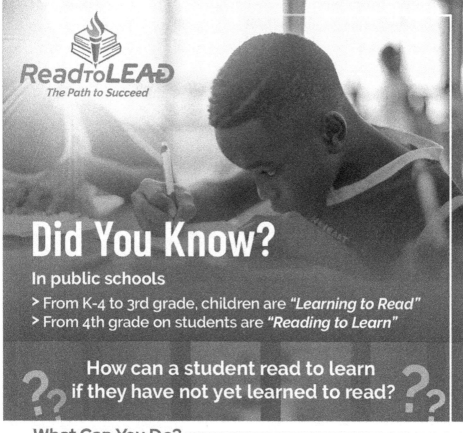